THE REDSHIFTING WEB

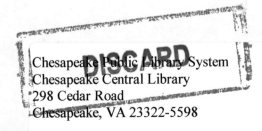

The Redshifting Web

POEMS 1970–1998

Arthur Sze

COPPER CANYON PRESS

Publication of this book is supported by a grant from the Lannan Foundation, the National Endowment for the Arts, and the Washington State Arts Commission, and by contributions from Elliott Bay Book Company, James Laughlin, and the members of the Friends of Copper Canyon Press. Copper Canyon Press is in residence with Centrum at Fort Worden State Park.

COVER ART: *Early Autumn*, detail, by Qian Xuan (1235–1305). Reproduced by permission of the Detroit Institute of Arts, Founders Society Purchase, General Membership Fund.

Library of Congress Cataloging-in-Publication Data
Sze, Arthur.
The redshifting web : poems 1970–1998 / by Arthur Sze.
p. cm.
ISBN 1-55659-088-1
I. Title.
PS3569.Z38 R44 1998
811'.54 – dc21 98-8920

COPPER CANYON PRESS
P.O. BOX 271, PORT TOWNSEND, WASHINGTON 98368

Grateful acknowledgment is made to the editors of the following publications in which these poems, sometimes in earlier versions, first appeared:

Alcatraz, The American Poetry Review, Archive Newsletter, Asian Pacific American Journal, B City, The Bloomsbury Review, Blue Unicorn, Bridge, Buttons, Caliban, Cedar Rock, Chelsea, La Confluencia, Contact II, Coyote's Journal, First Intensity, Floating Island, The Greenfield Review, Hanging Loose, Harvard Magazine, High Plains Literary Review, The Kenyon Review, Kyoto Journal, Longhouse, Manoa, Mill Mountain Review, Mother Jones, New Letters, New Letters Reader II, El Palacio, The Paris Review, Pax, Pharos, Puerto del Sol, Quarry West, Read Street, River Styx, Salted in the Shell, San Marcos Review, The Seattle Review, Sonora Review, Spazio Umano, The Sunstone Review, The Taos Review, Tendril, Tonantzin, 2 Plus 2, Tyuonyi; *America in Poetry* (Harry N. Abrams), *American Poets Say Goodbye to the Twentieth Century* (Four Walls Eight Windows Press), *Another Way to Dance* (Tsar), *Anthology of Magazine Verse and Yearbook of American Poetry* (Monitor), *Articulations* (University of Iowa Press), *Breaking Silence* (Greenfield Review Press), *Chinese American Poetry* (Asian American Voices), *Crossing the River* (Permanent Press), *Despite This Flesh* (University of Texas Press), *The Forgotten Language* (Peregrine Smith), *The Gift of Tongues* (Copper Canyon), *I Feel A Little Jumpy Around You* (Simon and Schuster), *The Indian Rio Grande* (San Marcos Press), *New Mexico Poetry Renaissance* (Red Crane Books), *The Open Boat* (Anchor/Doubleday), *Poems for the Wild Earth* (Blackberry), *The Practice of Peace* (Sherman Asher), *Premonitions* (Kaya Production), *Probes* (Macmillan), *Pushcart Prize XXI* (Pushcart Press), *The San Francisco Bark* (Thorp Springs Press), *Sparks of Fire* (North Atlantic Books), *The Statement of Two Rivers* (Shanghai Literature and Arts Publishing House), and *Today* (Oxford University Press).

The Willow Wind was first published in 1972 by Rainbow Zenith Press; second edition, revised, Tooth of Time Books, 1981. *Two Ravens* was first published in 1976 by Tooth of Time Books; second edition, revised, Tooth of Time Books, 1984. *Dazzled* was first published by Floating Island Publications, 1982. *River River* was first published by Lost Roads Publishers, 1987. *Archipelago* was first published by Copper Canyon Press, 1995. I wish to thank the poets who first published these books: John Brandi, Michael Sykes, Forrest Gander and C. D. Wright, and Sam Hamill. I also wish to thank everyone at Copper Canyon Press for their support.

In the opening section, new poems first appeared in the following publications: *Colorado Review*: "The Architecture of Silence," "Diffraction Grating"; *Columbia*: "Hourglass"; *Conjunctions*: "The String Diamond"; *Denver Quarterly*: "The Names of a Bird"; *Frank* (Paris): "Anamnesis," "Reductions and Enlargements," "Starlight"; *Manoa*: "Before Completion," "*Kaiseki*"; *New Letters*: "The Beginning Web"; *Orion*: "Apache Plume"; *The Poets' Calendar* (Sun & Moon Press): "Entelechy."

I am grateful to the Lila Wallace–Reader's Digest Fund for a Lila Wallace–Reader's Digest Writers' Award (1997); the Before Columbus Foundation for an American Book Award (1996); the Lannan Foundation for a Lannan Literary Award for Poetry (1995); the John Simon Guggenheim Memorial Foundation (1997), the Witter Bynner Foundation for Poetry (1980, 1983, 1994), the National Endowment for the Arts (1982, 1993), and the George A. and Eliza Gardner Howard Foundation at Brown University (1991) for fellowships; the New Mexico Arts Division for an inter-disciplinary grant (1988); the Santa Fe Council for the Arts for NEA writers-in-residence grants (1979, 1980, 1982); and the University of California at Berkeley for the Eisner Prize (1971). I wish to thank Frank Stewart, Jeanie Kim, Patrick Lannan, Steven Schwartz, David Berry, and Sheila Murphy for their support.

For Micah

CONTENTS

New Poems

FROM *The Willow Wind* (1972)

FROM *Two Ravens* (1976)

Dazzled (1982)

*

River River (1987)

NEW POEMS

BEFORE COMPLETION

1 I gaze through a telescope at the Orion Nebula,
a blue vapor with a cluster of white stars,
gaze at the globular cluster in Hercules,
needle and pinpoint lights stream into my eyes.
A woman puts a baby in a plastic bag
and places it in a dumpster; someone
parking a car hears it cry and rescues it.
Is this the little o, the earth?
Deer at dusk are munching apple blossoms;
a green snake glides down flowing acequia water.
The night is rich with floating pollen;
in the morning, we break up the soil
to prepare for corn. Fossilized cotton pollen
has been discovered at a site above six thousand feet.
As the character *yi*, change, is derived
from the skin of a chameleon, we are
living the briefest hues on the skin
of the world. I gaze at the Sombrero Galaxy
between Corvus and Spica: on a night with no moon,
I notice my shadow by starlight.

2 Where does matter end and space begin?

blue jays eating suet;

juggling three crumpled newspaper balls
wrapped with duct tape;

tasseling corn;

the gravitational bending of light;

"We're dying";

stringing a coral necklace;

he drew his equations on butcher paper;

vanishing in sunlight;

sobbing;

she folded five hundred paper cranes and placed them in a
basket;

sleeping in his room in a hammock;

they drew a shell to represent zero;

red persimmons;

what is it like to catch up to light?

he threw Before Completion:
six in the third place, nine in the sixth.

3 A wavering line of white-faced ibises,
flying up the Rio Grande, disappears.
A psychic says, "Search a pawnshop

for the missing ring." Loss, a black hole.
You do not intend to commit a series of
blunders, but to discover in one error

an empty cocoon. A weaver dumps
flashlight batteries into a red-dye bath.
A physicist says, "After twenty years,

nothing is as I thought it would be."
You recollect watching a yellow-
and-black-banded caterpillar in a jar

form a chrysalis: in days the chrysalis
lightened and became transparent:
a monarch emerged and flexed its wings.

You are startled to retrieve what you forgot:
it has the crunching sound of river
breakup when air is calm and very clear.

4 Beijing, 1985: a poet describes herding pigs
beside a girl with a glass eye and affirms
the power to dream and transform. Later,
in exile, he axes his wife and hangs himself.
Do the transformations of memory
become the changing lines of divination?
Is the continuum of a moment a red
poppy blooming by a fence, or is it
a woman undergoing radiation treatment
who stretches out on a bed to rest
and senses she is stretching out to die?
At night I listen to your breathing,
guess at the freckles on your arms,
smell your hair at the back of your neck.
Tiger lilies are budding in pots in the patio;
daikon is growing deep in the garden.
I see a bewildered man ask for direction,
and a daikon picker points the way with a daikon.

5 He threw Duration;

sunspots;

what is it like to catch up to light?

a collapsing vertebra;

the folding wings of a blue dragonfly;

receiving a fax;

buffeted on a floatplane between islands;

a peregrine falcon making a slow circle with outstretched
wings;

he crumpled papers, threw them on the floor,
called it City of Bums;

polar aligning;

inhaling the smell of her hair;

a red handprint on a sandstone wall;

digging up ginseng;

carding wool;

where does matter end and space begin?

6 Mushroom hunting at the ski basin, I spot
a blood-red amanita pushing up under fir,
find a white-gilled Man On Horseback,
notice dirt breaking and carefully unearth
a cluster of gold chanterelles. I stop
and gaze at yellow light in a clearing.
As grief dissolves and the mind begins to clear,
an s twist begins to loosen the z twisted fiber.
A spider asleep under a geranium leaf
may rest a leg on the radial string of a web,
but cool nights are pushing nasturtiums to bloom.
An eggplant deepens in hue and drops to the ground.
Yellow specks of dust float in the clearing;
in memory, a series of synchronous spaces.
As a cotton fiber burns in an s twist
and unravels the z twist of its existence,
the mind unravels and ravels a wave of light,
persimmons ripening on leafless trees.

O

THE STRING DIAMOND

1 An apricot blossom opens to five petals.
You step on a nail, and, even as you wince,
a man closes a mailbox, a cook sears
shredded pork in a wok, a surgeon sews
a woman up but forgets to remove a sponge.
In the waiting room, you stare at a diagram
and sense compression of a nerve where
it passes through the wrist and into the hand.
You are staring at black and white counters
on a crisscrossed board and have no idea
where to begin. A gardener trims chamisa
in a driveway; a roofer mops hot tar;
a plumber asphyxiates in a room with
a faulty gas heater; a mechanic becomes
an irrational number and spirals into himself.
And you wonder what inchoate griefs
are beginning to form? A daykeeper sets
a random handful of seeds and crystals into lots.

2 Pin a mourning cloak to a board and observe
brown in the wings spreading out to a series

of blue circles along a cream-yellow outer band.
A retired oceanographer remembers his father

acted as a double agent during the Japanese occupation,
but the Kuomintang general who promised a pardon

was assassinated; his father was later sentenced
as a collaborator to life in prison, where he died.

Drinking snake blood and eating deer antler
is no guarantee the mind will deepen and glow.

You notice three of the four corners of an intersection
are marked by ginkgo, horse chestnut, cluster

of pear trees, and wonder what the significance is.
Is the motion of a red-dye droplet descending

in clear water the ineluctable motion of a life?
The melting point of ice is a point of transparency,

as is a kiss, or a leaf beginning to redden,
or below a thunderhead lines of rain vanishing in air.

3 Deltoid spurge,
red wolf,
ocelot,
green-blossom pearlymussel,
razorback sucker,
wireweed,
blunt-nosed leopard lizard,
mat-forming quillwort,
longspurred mint,
kern mallow,
Schaus swallowtail,
pgymy madtom,
relict trillium,
tan riffleshell,
humpback chub,
large-flowered skullcap,
black lace cactus,
tidewater goby,
slender-horned spineflower,
sentry milk-vetch,
tulotoma snail,
rice rat,
blowout penstemon,
rough pigtoe,
marsh sandwort,
snakeroot,
scrub plum,
bluemask darter,
crested honeycreeper,
rough-leaved loosestrife.

4 In the mind, an emotion dissolves into a hue;
there's the violet haze when a teen drinks
a pint of paint thinner, the incarnadined
when, by accident, you draw a piece of
Xerox paper across your palm and slit
open your skin, the yellow when you hear
they have dug up a four-thousand-year-old
corpse in the Taklamakan Desert,
the scarlet when you struggle to decipher
a series of glyphs which appear to
represent sunlight dropping to earth
at equinoctial noon, there's the azure
when the acupuncturist son of a rabbi
extols the virtues of lentils, the brown
when you hear a man iced in the Alps
for four thousand years carried dried
polypores on a string, the green when
ravens cry from the tops of swaying spruces.

5 The first leaves on an apricot, a new moon,
a woman in a wheelchair smoking in a patio,
a CAT scan of a brain: these are the beginnings
of strings. The pattern of black and white
stones never repeats. Each loss is particular:
a gold ginkgo leaf lying on the sidewalk,
the room where a girl sobs. A man returns
to China, invites an old friend to dinner,
and later hears his friend felt he missed
the moment he was asked a favor and was
humiliated; he tells others never to see
this person from America, "He's cunning, ruthless."
The struggle to sense a nuance of emotion
resembles a chrysalis hanging from a twig.
The upstairs bedroom filling with the aroma
of lilies becomes a breathing diamond.
Can a chrysalis pump milkweed toxins into wings?
In the mind, what never repeats? Or repeats endlessly?

6 Dropping circles of gold paper,
before he dies,
onto Piazza San Marco;

  pulling a U-turn
  and throwing the finger;

a giant puffball
filling the car
with the smell of almonds;

  a daykeeper pronounces the day,
  "Net";

slits a wrist,
writes the characters "revolt"
in blood on a white T-shirt;

  a dead bumblebee
  in the greenhouse;

the flaring tail of a comet,
dessicated vineyard,
tsunami;

  a ten-dimensional
  form of go;

slicing abalone on the counter –
sea urchins
piled in a Styrofoam box;

honeydew seeds
germinating in darkness.

7 A hummingbird alights on a lilac branch
and stills the mind. A million monarchs
may die in a frost? I follow the wave
of blooming in the yard: from iris to
wild rose to dianthus to poppy to lobelia
to hollyhock. You may find a wave in
a black-headed grosbeak singing from a cottonwood
or in listening to a cricket at dusk.
I inhale the smell of your hair and see
the cloud of ink a cuttlefish releases in water.
You may find a wave in a smoked and
flattened pig's head at a Chengdu market,
or in the diamond pulse of a butterfly.
I may find it pulling yarn out of an indigo vat
for the twentieth time, watching the yarn
turn dark, darker in air. I find it
with my hand along the curve of your waist,
sensing in slow seconds the tilt of the Milky Way.

O

KAISEKI

1 An aunt has developed carpal tunnel syndrome
from using a pipette. During the Cultural Revolution,
she was tortured with sleep deprivation. Some
of the connections in her memory dissolved
into gaps. "My mind has leaps now," she says,
as she reaches for bean threads in a boiling pot.
Her son recollects people lined up to buy
slices of cancerous tripe. "If you boil it,
it's edible," he says. And a couple who ate
a destroying angel testified it was delicious –
they had not intended to become love suicides.
What are the points of transformation in a life?
You choose three green Qianlong coins and throw
"Corners of the Mouth," with no changing lines.
You see red and green seaweed washing onto
smooth black stones along a rocky shoreline,
sense the moment when gravity overtakes light
and the cosmos stops expanding and begins to contract.

2 In the Brazos, he has never found a matsutake
under ponderosa pine, but in the dark

he whiffs it pungent white. Five votive candles
are lined along the fireplace; she has lit

a new candle even though the one burning
holds days of light. The night-blooming cereus

by the studio window is budding from rain.
In his mind, he sees the flyswatter

hanging from a nail on the lintel, a two-eyed
Daruma hanging from the rearview mirror of the car.

He hears the dipping and rising pitch of a siren
glide up the street and senses a shift

in starlight, the Horsehead Nebula, and, in the dark,
her eyelashes closing and opening on his skin.

3 He knew by the sound that the arrow was going to miss the
target;

pins floating on water;

I saw the collapsing rafters in flames;

the dark side of the moon;

if *p* then *q*;

simplicity is to complexity
as a photon is to a hummingbird?

fire turns to what is dry;

when the Chinese woman wore a blond wig,
people grew uneasy;

an egg exploding in a microwave;

morels pushing up through burned ground;

at the cash register,
Siamese fighting fish were stacked in small glass bowls;

she lost all her hair;

digging up truffles;

what is "a quantum unit of light"?

4 *Tokpela*: sky: the first world; in her mind,
she has designed an exhibit exemplifying
Hopi time and space. He sees the white sash
with knots and strands hanging from the *trastero*.
He sees the wild rose by the gate, knows
red nasturtiums are blooming by the kitchen door.
She is pressing the blender button and grinding
cochineal bugs into bits; she is sorting
slides of Anasazi textile fragments on a light board.
He recalls when they let loose a swarm
of ladybugs in the yard. It is light-years
since she wove a white manta on the vertical loom,
light years since they walked out together
to the tip of Walpi and saw the San Francisco Peaks.
Goldfish swim in the pond in the back garden.
The night-blooming cereus opens five white blossoms
in a single night. He remembers looking
through a telescope at craters, and craters
inside craters on the moon. He recalls
being startled at the thought, gravity precedes light.

5 They searched and searched for a loggerhead shrike;

"I can't believe how you make me come" –
she knew he was married
but invited him to the opera;

diving for sea urchins;

the skin of a stone;

"You asshole!"

the nuclear trigrams were identical;

the wing beats of a crow;

maggots were crawling inside the lactarius cap;
for each species of mushroom,
a particular fly;

a broad-tailed hummingbird
whirred at an orange nasturtium;

"Your time has come";

opening the shed with a batten;

p if and only if *q*;

he put the flyswatter back on the nail.

6 The budding chrysanthemums in the jar have the color
of dried blood. Once, as she lit a new candle,

he asked, "What do you pray for?" and remembered
her earlobe between his teeth but received a gash

when she replied, "Money." He sees the octagonal
mirror at a right angle to the fuse box, sees

the circular mirror nailed into the bark of the elm
at the front gate and wonders why the obsession

with *feng shui*. He sees the photograph of a weaver
at a vertical loom kneeling at an unfinished

Two Grey Hills and wonders, is she weaving or unweaving?
The candlelight flickers at the bottom of the jar.

He sees back to the millisecond the cosmos was pure energy
and chooses to light a new candle in her absence.

7 I plunge enoki mushrooms into simmering broth
and dip them in wasabi, see a woman remove
a red-hot bowl from a kiln and smother it in sawdust.
I see a right-hand petroglyph with concentric
circles inside the palm, and feel I am running
a scrap of metal lath across a drying coat of cement.
I eat sea urchin roe and see an orange starfish
clinging below the swaying waterline to a rock.
I am opening my hands to a man who waves
an eagle feather over them, feel the stretch
and stretch of a ray of starlight. This
black raku bowl with a lead-and-stone glaze
now has the imprint of tongs. I dip raw blowfish
into simmering sake on a brazier, see a lover
who combs her hair and does not know she is humming.
I see a girl crunching on chips at the laundromat,
sense the bobbing red head of a Mexican finch.
Isn't this the most mysterious of all possible worlds?

8 A heated stone on a white bed of salt –

sleeping on a subway grate –

a thistle growing in a wash –

sap oozing out of the trunk of a plum –

yellow and red roses hanging upside down under a skylight –

fish carcasses at the end of a spit –

two right hands on a brush drawing a dot then the character,
water –

an ostrich egg –

a coyote trotting across the street in broad daylight –

sharpening a non-photo blue pencil –

the scar at a left wrist –

a wet sycamore leaf on the sidewalk –

lighting a kerosene lamp on a float house –

kaiseki: breast stones: a Zen meal –

setting a yarrow stalk aside to represent the infinite –

9 They threw "Pushing Upward" –

the pearl on a gold thread dangling at her throat –

a rice bowl with a splashed white slip –

biting the back of her neck –

as a galaxy acts as a gravitational lens and bends light –

stirring *matcha* to a froth with a bamboo whisk –

brushing her hair across his body –

noticing a crack
has been repaired with gold lacquer –

the Hyakutake Comet's tail flaring upward in the April sky –

orange and pink entwined bougainvilleas blooming in a pot –

"Oh god, oh my god," she whispered and began to glow –

yellow tulips opening into daylight –

staring at a black dot on the brown iris of her right eye –

water flows to what is wet.

O

APACHE PLUME

1 THE BEGINNING WEB

Blue flax blossoming near the greenhouse
is a luminous spot, as is a point south

of the Barrancas where two rivers join.
By the cattail pond, you hear dogs

killing a raccoon. In mind, these spots
breathe and glow. In the bath I pour

water over your shoulder, notice the spot
where a wild leaf has grazed your skin.

I see the sun drop below the San Andres
Mountains, white dunes in starlight;

in the breathing chiaroscuro, I glimpse
red-winged blackbirds nesting in the cattails,

see a cow pushing at the wobbly point
in a fence. In this beginning web of light,

I feel the loops and whorls of your fingertips,
hear free-tailed bats swirling out into the dark.

2 REDUCTIONS AND ENLARGEMENTS

A Chippewa designer dies from pancreatic cancer
and leaves behind tracing paper, Exacto knives,

rubber cement, non-photo blue pencils,
a circular instrument that calculates reductions

and enlargements. A child enters a house and finds
a dead man whose face has been eaten by dogs.

Who is measuring the pull of the moon in a teacup?
In a thousand years, a man may find barrels

of radioactive waste in a salt bed and be unable
to read the warnings. Sand is accumulating

at the bottom of an hourglass, and anything –
scissors, green wind chime, pencil shavings,

eraser smudge, blooming orchid under skylight –
may be a radial point into light. When a carp

flaps its tail and sends ripples across the surface
of a pond, my mind steadies into a glow. Look

at a line that goes into water, watch the wake,
see the string pulse and stretch into curved light.

3 THE NAMES OF A BIRD

You find a downy woodpecker on the bedroom floor.
I am startled and listen in the snowy dark

to deer approach a house and strip yew leaves.
In pots, agapanthuses are opening umbels

of violet flowers. Neither driven by hunger
nor flowering in the moment, what drives an oologist

to distinguish finch eggs from wren or sparrow?
What drives a physicist to insist the word

sokol means *falcon* in Hungarian? If you know
the names of a bird in ten languages, do you know

any more about the bird? Driving past an ostrich farm,
I recollect how you folded a desert willow blossom

into a notebook; I recollect rolling down
a white dune at dusk, pulling a green jade disk

on a thread at your throat into my mouth.
I know what it is to touch the mole between your breasts.

The gate was unlocked. We drove to the road's end; grapefruit lay on the ground not far from a white house whose window caught a glare. December 29, four P.M. At first we couldn't find the trail but walked ahead and crossed a river full of black boulders. Days earlier, we had looked down into the valley from a *kukui* grove. There was speckled bark, slanting rain, horses in a field, drenching rain. We had been walking back from the ocean where we moved from rock to rock and saw black crabs scuttling along the tide line. We looked into the water, saw sea cucumbers on rocks. On the way back, white lepiotas among grass and a small white puffball. I sliced open the puffball, but it was olive-green. Deer, crossing the road, stopped near the fence line and gazed back at us. I inhaled the aroma of shredded ginger and saw three pairs of dragonflies overhead, their wings catching daylight. Where is the one inside the many? Or are there many inside one? We came to a fork in the trail and noticed an exposed root growing across the right fork. We twisted left and glimpsed twin waterfalls; wild boar were stunned in our headlights. In the twilight, we came to another stream with white water rushing across black boulders and paused:

raindrops
dropping off the eaves
stop dropping

5 HOURGLASS

Père Lachaise: breaking bread on a green bench
under chestnut trees as rain drizzles down the leaves
and smoke rises out of the crematorium chimney –

is recollection a form of memento mori?
I see papyrus growing in a copper tub in the bedroom;
your hands rub blackthorn oil into my skin.

I close my eyes, feel the warmth of straw-flecked adobe walls –
a white chrysanthemum opens in a cup of boiling water.
Willow leaves on the skylight cast onto an ocher wall

shadows resembling herring under a float house.
Is recollection a form of epistemological inquiry?
I am cradling you as you lean back into me,

flecks of white sand in your hair and on your eyelids.
I am holding you in a white dune as the moon rises,
as white sand begins to touch the bottom of an hourglass.

6 ENTELECHY

Placing long-stemmed sunflowers in a vase
or staring at a map of Paris

may be forms of ripening.
In the garden, red-leaf lettuce has bolted in the heat.

The surface of water in an old whiskey barrel
twitches with mosquito larvae.

A bingo billboard on a highway
may be a momentary rippling,

but the deeper undulation is shark-womb skin.
Slicing abalone on the counter,

I catch a tidal surge at my fingertips.
By candlelight, a yellow cosmos,

koi roiling the surface of a stream into gold flecks,
your sharp wild cries.

7 APACHE PLUME

Climbing out of an arroyo, I reach my hand
into a small cactus and see the taro

plant in the backyard unfurl a new leaf.
A great horned owl perched on a ledge

twitches its ears when we approach along
the bottom of a ravine. I spot a hummingbird

at the hollyhock, pear blossoms swirling
on gravel near the gate. When you light

a candle, the flickering shadow on the wall
has the shape of an eagle feather.

In the morning when you do a yoga stretch,
I feel the rhythm with which you sway –

fingertip to fingertip, mouth to mouth,
the shifting course of the Pojoaque River,

white apache plume blossoming to silvery puff.
And as an astronomer catches light echoes

from a nova, when I pull spines out of my palm,
I know this instant moment which is ours.

8 ANAMNESIS

Wind erases our footprints on a transverse dune.
A yellow yolk of sun drops below the horizon

as a white moon rises. Claret cup cactus
blooms in white sand, while soaptree yuccas

move as a dune moves. The mind reduces a pond
to a luminous green speck and enlarges

a flecked amanita muscaria cap into a cosmos.
Running my hand along the curve of your waist,

I wonder if knowledge is a form of anamnesis.
When I pour warm water down your spine,

a boletus barrowsii releases spores into air.
As a stone drops into a pool and red koi

swim toward the point of impact, we set
a yarrow stalk aside and throw "Duration,"

glimpse a spiral of bats ascending out of a cave;
one by one they flare off into indigo air.

9 STARLIGHT

Here skid marks on I-25 mark a head-on collision;

here I folded an origami crane;

here a man writes in grass style: *huan wo he shan*;

here black poplar leaves swayed on the surface of clearest water;

here a downy woodpecker drills high in the elm;

here a dog drags a horse's leg back from the arroyo;

here Keene cement burned into my wrist and formed a riparian
scar;

here, traveling at night through the Sonoran Desert,
everyone choked when sand swept through the open windows
of the train;

here yellow and red ranunculi unfold under a chandelier;

here in the Jemez Mountains a cluster of *clitocybe dilata*;

here we spot eleven dolphins swimming between kelp beds up
the coast;

here we look through binoculars at the blue ion tail of a comet
in the northwest sky;

here pelicans are gliding above a cliff;

here when I pour water down the drain, a black cricket pops up;

here the first thing I saw when I opened my eyes
was a cut peony in a glass;

here is the origin of starlight.

10 DIFFRACTION GRATING

Sipping kava out of a tea bowl,
I am descending into a cavern that inhales

and exhales once each day. I see an alula
in a tropical greenhouse, the tracks

a bleached earless lizard makes in white sand,
the tracks my fingers make on your skin.

I see a spectrum of origami cranes
strung on thread at a Kurashiki temple,

Manchurian cranes in a cage and a salt
sumo ring. Papyrus stalks arc out of an urn

near the fireplace on the bedroom floor.
Is a solar flare a form of a koan?

Blue larkspur in a glass vase.
A stalactite dripping into a pool of water.

Hush: there is nothing in ten dimensions
that is not dilating the pupils of our eyes.

SIX PERSIMMONS

1 "*Cabron*," rings in his ears as he walks down
the corridor to death row. Where is the epicenter
of a Los Angeles earthquake? Hypocenter of "Fat Man"?
He watches a woman pour honey into a jar crammed
with psilocybin mushrooms. A few cells down,
a priest intones and oozes black truffles in olive oil.
He is about to look at the poems of a murderer,
sees a sliced five-thousand-year-old silkworm cocoon.
x: pinhole, eclipse; the, a; shadow of mosquito,
fern frond uncoiling in mist. "Dot," says a Japanese
calligrapher who draws a dot beginning on the floor
off the page. He looks at the page, shrugs,
there is nothing there, and pictures budding chamisa
in a courtyard, yellow yarrow hanging over a bed.
In Waimea Canyon, *'apapane*, *'i'iwi*. x: it's
the shapes of ice in an ice floe, a light-green
glazed lotus-shaped hot-water bowl. He opens his eyes
and recalls staring into her eyes as she comes.

2 A visual anthropologist dies in a head-on collision
and leaves behind an Okinawan bow, whisk,
Bizen bowl, hammock, New Guinea coffee beans,
calligraphic scroll, "In motion there is stillness."
Walking along the shifting course of the Pojoaque River,
I ponder the formation of sunspots, how they appear
to be floating islands, gigantic magnetic storms
on the surface of the sun, and, forming cooler regions,
become darker to the human eye. I ponder how
he slowed the very sharpening of a pencil
but sped up La Bajada behind a semi in the dark,
and, when the semi shifted into the right lane,
was sandwiched and smashed into an out-of-state
pickup driving down the wrong side of the highway.
I hold the blued seconds when – Einstein Cross –
he cursed, slammed on the brakes – the car crunched
and flew apart in a noise he could not hear into
a pungent white saguaro blossom opening for a single night.

3 Green dragonflies hover over water. In the mind,
the axis of absence and presence resembles
a lunar eclipse. Hiking a ridge trail in the Barrancas,
we notice the translucent wing feathers of
a red-tailed hawk circling overhead. Once,
inadvertently, I glanced out the bathroom window
and noticed yellow yarrow blooming in sunshine.
A man does not have to gamble his car away
and hitchhike out of Las Vegas for the mind to ripen.
Bill Isaacs slices an agaricus lengthwise, points
to the yellow base of stipe, says, "Xanthodermus."
Although he has walked up a trail into spruce
and fir, mycelium in his hands has spread out.
Although asthma may be passed from one to another,
one mind may be a sieve, while the other may be
crystals growing up a string. Is sun to earth to moon
as mind to shiitake to knife? When one mind
passes to another, green dragonflies hover over water.

4 Is the recollecting mind an aviary? Once he pushed
through hermetically sealed revolving doors
into a humid forest where he sighted a toucan,
but where is the *o'o a'a*? A pin fits in a pocket,
but how do you put a world inside a world?
Two twins, ex-marines, stretch Okinawan bows
and aim their hips and eyes at the target;
the arrows are not yet not yet released.
As death burns a hole into a piece of paper,
a fern frond in the Alaka'i Swamp uncoils in mist.
He glows when she puts her hand on his chest;
the sun spins faster at the equator than at the poles.
He lays six blossoming orchid branches on the floor,
stares at the shapes of flower vases on shelves
in the storeroom. It is as if all the possible shapes
of the world were waiting to come into being,
as if a new shape was about to come into being,
when, x, a calico cat scratches at the door.

5

When you stoop to examine a lichen but find
alongside, barely exposed, several gold chanterelles,
I bend to earth in my mind: observe striations
along a white cap, absence of annulus, dig,
unearth a volva. We go on in the woods
and stumble into a cluster of teeth fungi
with dark upturned scales on their caps.
Who notices in the early morning Saturn slip
behind a waning gibbous moon? This year,
a creation spiral slowly incandesces in my hand.
I slip a white elastic band off and loosen
your hair, rub my thumb in your palm. I love
when wet sunlight splashes your face, recall
grilling shrimp near a corner of the screened porch
while rain slants across the field. In the few
weeks of a year when blood-red amanitas push
out of the earth, we push into a splendor of
yellow plumeria, orange hibiscus, bird of paradise.

6 Pears ripen in a lacquer bowl on the butcher-
block table. A red shimmer arcs across
the northwest sky as a galaxy bends the light
of a quasar. Yellow ranunculi unfold in a glass vase
while fireflies blink in a corner of the yard.
A physicist employs lasers and slows atoms
down to approach absolute zero; a calligrapher
draws the silk radical twice, then *mountain,*
to form "the most shady recesses in the hills."
As the ink dries, she lights two red candles
in the bedroom, notices near the curtains
taro in the huge tin tub, and spots a curling leaf.
He hears the gasp when he first unzipped
her jeans, knows the small o is a lotus seed
slowly germinating in his mind, but the
brevity of equation makes him quiver and ache.
When they turn to each other in a wet kiss,
their fingertips glow in the skin of their days.

from THE WILLOW WIND (1972)

NOAH'S / DOVE

The moon is black.
Had I a bird
it would fly,
beat the air into land.
To remain
or trust
the silver leaves of the sea?
What if
I say what *is*:
no bird, no land.
The sea tossing
its damp wet fish
on the bow,
their lungs exhaling
the sea, taking in
moon air
for the first time…

THE WOOD WHITTLER

Whales and fish
sailing
in the sky!

Old saws! Old saws!
Red flakes
falling off the wood

like leaves.
Fire?
The woodcutter

pares the skin
with a
knowing hand.

The blade – rude –
will carve
his / mind's mastery

in the /
witless earth.

LI PO

Jarred.
  The oars creaked in their locks.
Fish beneath the moon.
Cradled his pen
filled with wine.
        A goddess stirred,
rocked the cradle of his boat,
let the silent fish know
a dreamer's silver hands were at work.

MIRACLES

His lens misses her,
the leaves cast double reflections
on the glass. The one
is his shadow; as he leans up
he discovers a new perspective,
a range he never considered.
The leaves, shaggy-edged,
twirl the light in their hands.
A new source; he must
pay his respects deftly.
They have his power.
He must acquaint them
with this peripheral vision –
the woman walking down the steps
is no longer his wife.

THE EXECUTION OF MAXIMILIAN

Muskets triggered a white smoke,
and it fell like snow,
soft death to purple eyes.
I saw the clean glint of the man's pants,
and knew what was coming,
hit the ground for the last time.

And the snow covered me like a corpse.
They mistook me for one
who had lain there a long time.
And they rushed on instead
to the crumpled body by the wall,
stuck their bayonets in
laughing, and jostled each other on the shoulder
like friends long unseen, now returned.

SOUND LAG

His glazed lips
moved slower
than the
movement of words.
Overhead, black clouds
were poised
in the sky,
then moved on.
In the real sky
they had
no place to go.

The air cooled to zero.
I look again at myself
in the mirror.
The veins of the dark trees
outside
vibrate.
Their song is, at least,
mine, but
I am engaged elsewhere.
I extend my hand
through the glass
into the living world.

SLIDING AWAY

Your hand rigid, curled into its final shape:
the rest of your body breathes.
The dark coals you pour on his grave
continue to breathe.
A snake slides through the
uneven grass
where it has cut a
name for
itself
by
sliding away.

STRAWBERRIES IN WOODEN BOWLS

You carry flowers in a jug of green wine,
and the smell is that of the first fires in autumn
when the leaves are blown into their reds and grays.

The sunlight rains through the glass.
As you reach across the table
the fences outside disappear.
The fields are green with their rain
and the wind curls the stars in the cold air.

You stand now, silent, in the window of light
and the milk you pour is glazed.
The strawberries in the wooden bowls
are half-covered with curdled milk.

THE OLIVE GROVE

Up on the hill
the morning moon washed clean.
Thin dogs no longer
leap in the sunlight,
and I walk, easily, up the path.
The gatekeeper snores
in his rocking chair,
and only the wind
keeps him moving.

Turning now through the yard
I recall his eyes.
The leaves tinged
with inevitable grays.
With one hand
I pluck the olives
off the white lattice.
Their thick skins
rinsed in the moonshine.

A SINGER WITH EYES OF SAND

A singer with eyes of sand they said –
the western wind
                                        sweeps me home,
and I am carrying you, my desert,
in my hands.

from TWO RAVENS (1976)

THE TAOIST PAINTER

He begins with charcoal and outlines
the yellow fringes of the trees.
Then he rubs in the stumps, black
and brown, with an uneasy motion
of his thumbs. Unlike trees in the north,
he says, I have the option of season.
And he paints the leaves in the upswing
of the wind, and the swans craning their necks.
But the sunlight moving in patches
obscures and clarifies his view.
When he walks off in silence
we look at his painting and stand
astonished to see how, in chiaroscuro,
the leaves drift to their death.

BRUEGHEL

The haystacks burned to black moss.
I tilted my head and leveled
the mound; saw three women walking
home in step, hefting hoes, and
weighted by sunlight on the blades.
Three men, of course, circled away,
heads concealed by hats, joking,
clearly drunk on harvest wine.
But then the pageant slipped off
without me; the horse loped across
the ridge, and the sickle mender
tuned his ears to the wind.

THE SILVER TRADE

You will hammer silver into a heart
and the dogs will leap and yell.
No one will stop you though, and
before you learn how the body dies,
will smelt earrings for fuel.

Nail my spine to wood. I cannot live.
Under the open sky the wind
whips the sunlight into stone.
I thread the few stars into a crown
and throw them behind the mountain.

HE WILL COME TO MY FUNERAL WITH A WHITE FLOWER

He will come to my funeral with a white flower
and spread the petals, unevenly, on my dress.
Then he will turn, walk down the aisle, and
raise his elbow, to accompany his invisible bride.
Oh, though he comes with me to the market
and we buy fruit and vegetables for dinner,
he is a hermit in the mountains, watching
the water and the sunlight on the green stones.
His hands skim the rise and fall, reshaping
the ridges, and making the bend a woman's thigh.
No one can ever be part of his village, don
palm leaves and wear an inscrutable smile.
When he says goodbye, I know the water in his eyes
has been falling for centuries.

THE WAKING

Blue plums in the pewter bowl –
may they wake wet in the earth the wren singing
and cull the sweetest violet.
But the children sleep secure in blankets.

I climbed by spinning arms and legs against walls,
awakened waist-deep in the water-well;
wrestled the black bull before an audience,
beat the wind without wings,
paced the steeds along pampas grass…

In the morning chill
I breathe moths in my cupped hands.

NORTH TO TAOS

The aspen twig
    or leaf will snap: bells in the wind,
and the hills, obsidian,
    as the stars wheeling halt;
        twig and bark curling in the fire
kindle clusters of sparks.
    Steer north, then, to Taos, where
        the river, running deeper, cuts a gorge,
    and at midnight the moon
waxes; minnows scatter
    at your step,
        the boat is moored to sky.

THREE A.M., IN WINTER

When I went to Zuni,
    my mind was a singing arrow; the black desert
was shining, and I flew,
    a green peyote bird, in the wind's eye...
It's three A.M., and
    the road to Zuni is buried in snow.
        Thinking of you, I taste green wine,
    I touch sparks, I fly.

LAMENT

Let me pick
olives in the moonlight.
Let me ride
a pale green horse.
Let me taste the autumn fires.
Or else,
let me die in a war.

WANG WEI

At my window
    the rain raves, raves about dying,
and does not
    hear in the bamboo
        a zither which, plucked,
inebriates the birds
    and brings closer to the heart
        the moon.

MORNING SHUTTERS

We extend arms
infinitely long
into the sunrise.

Then the shutters close,
and we begin
the slow, painful
step of learning
shadows in the dark.

My hand goes to your thigh.
The hills
high above us
shine in the heat.

Now, the whites of your eyes
are filled
with the lost years.

LUPINE

I planted lupine and nasturtiums
in the dark April dirt. Who heard the passing
cars or trucks? I was held

by your face, eclipsed, in partial light.
I sip hibiscus tea, and am at peace
now in the purple dusk.

"Kwan, kwan," cries a bird, distant,
in the pines.

DO NOT SPEAK KERESAN TO A MESCALERO APACHE

Do not speak
Keresan to a Mescalero Apache,
but cultivate
private languages;

a cottonwood
as it disintegrates into gold,
or a house
nailed into the earth:

the dirt road
into that reservation
is unmarked.

DAZZLED (1982)

VIEWING PHOTOGRAPHS OF CHINA

Viewing photographs of China,
we visit a pearl farm, factories, and
watch a woman stare at us ten
minutes after a surgical operation
with acupuncture.
                                        The mind
is a golden eagle. An arctic tern
is flying in the desert: and
the desert incarnadined, the sun
incarnadined.
                                The photograph
of a poster of Chang Ch'ing is
two removes from reality. Lin Piao,
Liu Shao-chi, and Chang Ch'ing
are either dead or disgraced.
The poster shows her in a loose
dress drinking a martini; the
issues of the Cultural Revolution
are confounded.
                                    And, in perusing
the photographs in the mind's eye,
we discern bamboo, factories,
pearls; and consider African wars,
the Russian Revolution, the
Tierra Amarilla Courthouse Raid.
And instead of insisting that
the world have an essence, we
juxtapose, as in a collage,
facts, ideas, images:
                                        the arctic

tern, the pearl farm, considerations
of the two World Wars, Peruvian
horses, executions, concentration
camps; and find, as in a sapphire,
a clear light, a clear emerging
view of the world.

THE MOON IS A DIAMOND

Flavio Gonzales, seventy-two, made jackhammer
heads during the War; and tells me
about digging ditches in the Depression
for a dollar a day. We are busy plastering
the portal, and stop for a moment
in the April sun. His wife, sick for
years, died last January and left a
legacy – a $5,000 hospital bill.
I see the house he built at fifteen:
the *ristras* of red chili hanging
in the October sun. He sings "Paloma
Blanca" as he works, then stops,
turns: "I saw the TV photos of the
landing on the moon. But it's all
lies. The government just went out
in the desert and found a crater.
Believe me, I know, I know the moon
is a diamond."

LISTENING TO A BROKEN RADIO

I The night is
a black diamond.
I get up at 5:30 to drive to Jemez pueblo,
and pass the sign at the bank
at 6:04, temperature 37.
And brood: a canyon wren, awake, in its nest in the black pines,
and in the snow.

II America likes
the TV news that shows you the
great winning catch in a football game.
I turn left
at the Kiska store.
And think of the peripatetic woman
who lives with all her possessions in a shopping cart,
who lives on Sixth Avenue and Eighth Street,
and who prizes and listens to her
broken radio.

MOENKOPI

Your father had gangrene and
had his right leg amputated, and now has diabetes
and lives in a house overlooking the
uranium mines.
The wife of the clown at Moenkopi
smashes in the windows of a car with an ax,
and threatens to shoot her husband
for running around with another woman.

A child with broken bones
is in the oxygen tent for the second time;
and the parents are concerned he
has not yet learned how to walk.
People mention these incidents
as if they were points on a chart depicting
uranium disintegration. It is all
accepted, all disclaimed.

We fly a kite over the electrical
lines as the streetlights go on:
the night is silver, and the night
desert is a sea. We walk back
to find your grandfather working in the dark,
putting in a post to protect peaches,
watering tomatoes, corn, beans – making them grow
out of sand, barren sand.

WRITTEN THE DAY I WAS TO BEGIN A RESIDENCY AT THE STATE PENITENTIARY

Inmates put an acetylene torch to another inmate's face,
seared out his eyes.
Others were tortured, lacerated with barbed wire,
knifed, clobbered with lead pipes.

I remember going to the state pen to see a performance of
  Beckett.
I see two inmates play Ham and Clov.
Clov lifts weights all day,
his biceps are huge.
And Ham, in a wheelchair with a bloody handkerchief,
dark purple shades,
is wheeled around and around
in a circle in the gym:
as guards watch, talk on walkie-talkies, slam doors,
as a television crew tapes segments.

I do not know whether these two inmates died or lived.
But they are now the parts they played:
locked in a scenario of bondage and desperate need,
needing each other to define themselves.

I tell myself to be open to all experience,
to take what is ugly and find something nourishing in it:
as penicillin may be found in green moldy bread,
or as, in the morning, a child of the earth
floating in a porcelain jar full of rainwater
is something astonishing.

But after the SWAT team has moved in and taken over
the flotsam and jetsam of a prison,
and the inmates are lined up and handcuffed to a chain-link
    fence,
I figure their chances, without people caring,
are "an ice cube's chance in hell."

JUNE GHAZAL

Is the sun a miner, a thief, a gambler,
an assassin? We think the world

is a gold leaf spinning down in silence
to clear water? The deer watch us in the blue leaves.

The sun shines in the June river. We flit
from joy to grief to joy as a passing

shadow passes? And we who think the sun a miner,
a thief, a gambler, an assassin,

find the world in a gold leaf spinning down
in silence to clear water.

O

DAZZLED

Reality
is like a contemporary string
quartet:

the first violinist puts on a crow's head.
And the cellist

soliloquizes on a white lotus
in the rain.

The violist discusses
love, rage, and terror.

And the second violinist reports on the latest coup
in Afghanistan.

A gazelle leaps
in October light.

I am dazzled.

MAGNETIZED

Jimson weed
has nothing to do
with the blueprint of a house,
or a white macaw.

But an iron bar,
magnetized, has a north and south
pole that attract.
Demagnetized, it has nothing
at either end.

The mind magnetizes
everything it touches.
A knife in a dog
has nothing to do
with the carburetor of an engine:

to all appearances,
to all appearances.

KNIFE AT THE JUGULAR

Sentenced to two consecutive
life terms, Robert Francis may be
paroled in twenty years. He may

walk out of jail at forty,
a free man. But the world travels
at the speed of light.

He will be a miner staggering
out of a collapsed mine. People
will have assumed he died

years ago. And, at forty,
the world will feel like *jamais*
vu. The barbed wire and

sunlight will be his only
friends. Perhaps, he will discern
freedom as a rat swimming in

a ditch, or pleasure as the
smell of green tea. And the full
moon, crazed with the voices

of dead men, will make him
relive again and again the double
ax murder. And will he know

himself? The Eskimos have
thirty words describing varieties
of ice. I see a man in

twenty years walking into the
sunlight. He will know a thousand
words for varieties of pain.

His first act may be a knife
at the jugular, and his ensuing acts
may be terrors of the earth.

POUILLY-FUISSÉ

1 Foxes and pheasants adorn
the store window. A woman sells
dried anise, dried purple

mallow, and caviar inside.
But we don't live on purple mallow,
or Pouilly-Fuissé. I think

of the Africans I met
going to pick grapes at
$1.40 an hour.

2 A man trying to sell roses
throws water, and, instead of sprinkling,
drenches the roses. And

an old woman carrying leeks
wears shoes at least three sizes too large,
and walks almost crippled.

But, then, they make a world of
leeks and roses.

ALBA

South light
wakes us. I turn
to your touch,
your long hair, and
slow kisses.
A wren sings in
the clear light.
Red cassia
blossoms in your
hands. And all
day the wren sings
in the day's
branches.

THE OPAL

Nailing up chicken wire on the frame house,
or using a chalk line, or checking a level at a glance
gets to be easy.
We install double-pane windows
pressurized with argon between the panes
for elevations over 4500′.
And use pick and shovel
to dig for the footing for the annex. Lay cinder blocks,
and check levels. Pour the cement floor, and
use wood float and steel trowel to finish the surface
as it sets.
Nailing into rough, dense, knotted
two-by-twelves, or using a chalk line to mark the locations
of the fire blocks, or checking the level of a
stained eight-by-ten window header gets to be
easier.
In nailing up chicken wire, we know
how to cut for the *canal*, pull the wire up over the
fire wall, make cuts for the corners, tuck it
around back, and nail two-head nails into the stud.
And when the footing is slightly uneven and we are
laying a first row of cinder blocks, know that a
small pebble under a corner often levels the top
to the row.
And, starting on rock lath, the various
stages of a house – cutting *vigas*, cleaning aspens for
latillas, installing oak doors, or plastering the
adobe wall – are facets of a cut opal.

PENTIMENTO

In sepia, I draw a face and hands,
a river, a hawk. When I read your letter,
and feel the silences, the slow

changes in perspective, in feeling,
I make a fresco – fading even as it's painted.
It's pentimento: knowing the original

sepia lines, and the changes:
the left hand in darkness, a face, effaced,
in fading light, and the right hand

pointing to a Giotto-blue river, a blue hawk,
in a moment of grace.

THE WEATHER SHIFTS

Unemployed, I recollect setting a plumb
line for the doorjambs to a house,
recollect nailing a rebar through two corbels
locked in a 60° angle into a post; and
smell unpicked cherries, fragrant,
in the dark rich earth. It is a pellucid
night in January: and the mind has its
own shifts in weather: a feel for light
from a star, or for a woman's voice,
a recognition of the world's greed,
of a death march on the Philippines, or
of being shot by an arrow dipped in curare.
Drinking tequila, I watch the moon
rise slowly over the black hills; a bird
sings, somewhere, out in the junipers.

O

JUNIPER FIRES

Juniper
fires burn in the crisp night.
I am inebriated
on juniper smoke. And as my mind clears,
I see a white crane standing, one-legged, in the snow.
And see clearly the
rocks, and shaggy pines, the winter moon, and
creek.

FROST

Notice each windowpane has a different
swirling pattern of frost etched on the glass.

And notice how slowly the sun melts
the glaze. It is indelible: a fossil of a fern,

or a coelacanth, or a derelict who
rummages in his pockets and pulls out a few

apple cores. Notice the peculiar
angle of light in the slow shift of sunrise.

Where is the whir of the helicopter?
The search for escaped convicts in the city?

Be amazed at the shine and the wet.
Simply to live is a joy.

BLACK LIGHTNING

A blind girl
stares at me,
then types out ten lines
in braille.

The air has a scent
of sandalwood and
arsenic; a night-blooming cereus
blooms on a dark path.

I look at the
short and long flow
of the lines:
and guess at garlic,
the sun, a silver desert rain,
and palms.

Or is it simply
about hands, a river of light,
the ear of a snail,
or rags?

And, stunned, I feel
the nerves of my hand flashing
in the dark, feel
the world as black
lightning.

PIRANHAS

piranhas
in a wine-dark river.
a radio station on antarctica sends messages
to outer space,
listens to quasars pulsing in the spiral nebula of andromeda.
a banker goes for a drive
in a red mercedes,
smokes black russian sobranie from england.
the sun
rides a red appaloosa to the gold mountains in the west;
then, incognito, shows up in questa:
wearing shades, carrying a geiger counter, and
prospecting for plutonium.
the history of the world
is in a museum in albania;
the price of admission is one dollar.
a kgb agent
has located trotsky's corpse,
and, under the guise of a gardener, enters his house
and breaks open his casket, and
shatters his cranium with an ice pick.
lepers
in a cathedral are staring up at the rose window.
o window of light:
we are falling
into a bottomless lake full of piranhas –
the piranhas, luminous, opalescent,
in the black water.
o paris, venice, moscow, buenos aires, saigon, kuala lumpur:
we are sailing up the wine-dark
river.

IMPRESSIONS OF THE NEW MEXICO LEGISLATURE

The lieutenant governor sits in the center
behind an oak desk. Below him, the reader of bills
reads at thirty miles per hour to pass or defeat
a bill depending on his cue.
                                                  One senator
talks on the phone to Miss Española; another, a thug,
opens his briefcase, takes out a bottle
of whiskey, a shot glass, and begins drinking.
Bills from various committees are meanwhile passed
without comment. Finally, a bill is introduced,
and the lieutenant governor asks that the
content be explained.
                                        A senator rises, speaks
into a microphone: "Bill 345-B is one of my most
important pieces of legislation. It commemorates
J. D. Arguello and H. R. Lucero who died last year
while firefighting. It also specifically commends
Victor de la Cruz who is now crippled."
                                                                    Another
senator rises, introduces a bill to change the
composition of the podiatrist's board. Two members
of the public are to be on it. The lieutenant
governor asks what the requirements for the public
are. One senator quips, "Athlete's foot," is
out of order, and is silenced.
                                                    The senators quickly
agree that one member of the public is sufficient.
The lieutenant governor says, "All those in favor
may say 'ay,' those opposed may raise their feet."

ırt.
:aine, and henna.

in the eucalyptus,

Pleiades.
ed in the rock

at Puyé: carved, perhaps, seven hundred
years ago. And, now, we touch the Pleiades.

For two weeks, seven hundred years,
cedar fires burn in my heart.

THE MURMUR

The doctor flicks on a light,
puts up the X rays of our three-day-old child,
and diagnoses a shunt between
left and right ventricle,
claims an erratic electrocardiogram test
confirms his findings. Your child,
he says, may live three to six weeks unless
surgery is performed.

Two days later, a pediatric cardiologist
looks at the same X rays and EKG test,
pronounces them normal,
and listens with disinterest to the murmur.
I think, then, of the birth:
mother and child in a caesarean,
the rush of blood in the umbilical cord
is a river pulsating with light.

And, as water rippling in a pond
ricochets off rocks, the network of
feelings between father and mother
and child is an ever-shifting web.
It is nothing on your doctor's X ray
scanner; but, like minerals lit up
under a black light, it is an iridescent
red and green and indigo.

THE CORONA

Knife-edge
days and shimmering nights.
Our child watches the shifting sunlight and leaves.
The world shimmers, shimmers.

Smoke goes up the flue,
and spins, unravels in the wind.
Something in me unravels after long thought.
And my mind flares:
as if the sun and moon lock in an eclipse,
and the sun's corona flares out.

It is a fire
out of gasoline and rags
that makes us take nothing for granted.
And it is love, spontaneous,
flaring,
that makes us feel
like a cougar approaching a doe in labor,
makes us pause and move on.

OLIVE NIGHT

The Jemez
Indians mention the Los Ojos bar.
I think of the Swiss
army practicing maneuvers in the Alps.
The world is a hit-and-run, an armed robbery, and a fight.
I think of the evening star.
And ripen, as an olive ripens, in a cool
summer night.

○

THE CLOUD CHAMBER

A neighbor
rejects chemotherapy and the hospital;
and, instead, writes
a farewell letter to all her friends
before she dies.

I look at a wasp nest;
and, in the maze of hexagons,
find a few
white eggs, translucent, revealing formed wasps,
but wasps never to be born.

A pi-meson in a cloud chamber
exists for a thousandth of a second,
but the circular track
it leaves on a film
is immortal.

EMPTY WORDS

He describes eagle feathers with his hands.
He signs the rustle of pine needles on a mountain
path in sunlight, the taste of green water,
herding sheep in a canyon, the bones of a horse bleached
in sunlight, purple thistles growing in red dirt,
locoweed in bloom.

My mind is like a tumbleweed rolling
in the wind, smashing against the windshields of cars,
but rolling, rolling until nothing is left.
I sit in the sunlight, eyes closed:
empty mind, empty hands. I am a
great horned owl hunting in a night with no moon.

And this Indian, deaf-mute, is like a Serbian
in a twenty-four-hour truck stop,
is a yellow sandhill crane lost in Albuquerque.
I see the red blooms of a nasturtium battered
in a hailstorm. I see the bleached white bones of a horse
at the bottom of a canyon. And I see his hands,
empty hands, and words, empty words.

TSANKAWI

The men hiked on a loop trail
past the humpbacked flute player and
a creation spiral petroglyph,
then up a ladder to the top of the mesa
and met the women there.

A flock of wild geese wheeled
in shifting formation over the mesa,
then flew south climbing higher and higher
and disappearing in clear sunlight.
The ceremony was simple: a blessing
of rings by "water which knows no
boundaries," and then a sprinkling of baskets
with blue cornmeal.

I write of this a week later
and think of Marie, who, at San Ildefonso,
opened the door to her house to us.
And we were deeply moved.
I hear these lines from the wedding:
"In our country, wind blows, willows live,
you live, I live, we live."

ANTARES

You point to
Antares.
The wind rustles the cottonwood leaves.
And the intermittent

rain sounds like a fifty-
string zither. A red lotus blossoms
in the air. And, touching you,
I am like light from

Antares. It has taken me light-
years to arrive.

THE OWL

The path was purple in the dusk.
I saw an owl, perched,
on a branch.

And when the owl stirred, a fine dust
fell from its wings. I was
silent then. And felt

the owl quaver. And at dawn, waking,
the path was green in the
May light.

THE CORNUCOPIA

Grapes grow up a difficult and
sloped terrain. A soft line of poplars
shimmer in the disappearing light.
At midnight, the poor move
into the train stations of Italy,
spread out blankets for the children,
and pretend to the police they have tickets
and are waiting for a train.

The statue of Bacchus is a contrast
with his right hand holding a shallow but
wine-brimming cup. His left hand
reaches easily into the cornucopia
where grapes ripen and burst open.
It is a vivid dream: to wake
from the statue's grace and life force
to the suffering in the streets.

But the truth is the cornucopia
is open to all who are alive,
who look and feel the world in
its pristine beauty – as a dragonfly
hovering in the sunlight over clear
water; and who feel the world
as a luminous world – as green plankton
drifting at night in the sea.

THE CHANCE

The blue-black mountains are etched
with ice. I drive south in fading light.
The lights of my car set out before
me, and disappear before my very eyes.
And as I approach thirty, the distances
are shorter than I guess? The mind
travels at the speed of light. But for
how many people are the passions
ironwood, ironwood that hardens and hardens?
Take the ex-musician, insurance salesman,
who sells himself a policy on his own life;
or the magician who has himself locked
in a chest and thrown into the sea,
only to discover he is caught in his own chains.
I want a passion that grows and grows.
To feel, think, act, and be defined
by your actions, thoughts, feelings.
As in the bones of a hand in an X ray,
I want the clear white light to work
against the fuzzy blurred edges of the darkness:
even if the darkness precedes and follows
us, we have a chance, briefly, to shine.

THE NETWORK

In 1861, George Hew sailed in a rowboat
from the Pearl River, China, across
the Pacific ocean to San Francisco.
He sailed alone. The photograph of him
in a museum disappeared. But, in the mind,
he is intense, vivid, alive. What is
this fact but another fact in a world
of facts, another truth in a vast network
of truths? It is a red maple leaf
flaming out at the end of its life,
revealing an incredibly rich and complex
network of branching veins. We live
in such a network: the world is opaque,
translucent, or, suddenly, lucid,
vibrant. The air is alive and hums
then. Speech is too slow to the mind.
And the mind's speech is so quick it breaks
the sound barrier and shatters glass.

FAUVE

Caw Caw, Caw Caw Caw.
To comprehend a crow
you must have a crow's mind.
To be the night rain,
silver, on black leaves,
you must live in the
shine and wet. Some people
drift in their lives:
green-gold plankton,
phosphorescent, in the sea.
Others slash: a knife
at a yellow window shade
tears open the light.
But to live digging deep
is to feel the blood
in you rage as rivers,
is to feel love and hatred
as fibers of a rope,
is to catch the scent
of a wolf, and turn wild.

FERN, COAL, DIAMOND

The intense pressure of the earth
makes coal out of ferns, diamonds out of coal.
The intense pressure of the earth
is within us, and makes coal
and diamond desires.

For instance, we are a river
flowing and flowing out to sea,
an oak fire flaring and flaring in a night
with no wind, or, protean,
a river, a fire, an oak, a hawk, a wind.

And now, at first light,
I mark the stages of our growth:
mark fern, coal, diamond,
mark a pressure transforming
even broken nails and broken glass into
clear molten light.

THE AXIS

I hear on the radio that Anastasio Somoza
has fled Managua, is already in Florida,

and about to disappear on a world cruise.
Investigators in this country are meanwhile

analyzing the volcanic eruptions on Io,
or are studying the erratic respiratory

pattern of a sea horse to find the origin
of life. The fact is, we know so little,

but are so quick to interpret, to fit facts
to our schemata. For instance, the final

collapse of the Nicaraguan dictatorship
makes me wonder if the process of change

is a dialectic. Or is our belief in a
pattern what sustains it? Is the recent

history a clear pattern: a dictatorship
followed by a popular revolt, followed by

a renewed dictatorship exercising greater
repression, ended by a violent revolution?

I want to speak of opposites that depend
on and define each other: as in a

conversation, you feel silence in speech,
or speech in silence. Or, as in a

counterpoint when two melodies overlap and
resonate, you feel the sea in the desert,

or feel that the body and mind are
inseparable. Then you wonder if day and

night are indeed opposites. You knock the
gyroscope off the axis of its spinning,

so that one orientation in the world vanishes
and the others appear infinite.

RIVER RIVER (1987)

THE LEAVES OF A DREAM ARE THE LEAVES OF AN ONION

1 Red oak leaves rustle in the wind.
Inside a dream, you dream the leaves
scattered on dirt, and feel it
as an instance of the chance configuration

to your life. All night you feel
red horses galloping in your blood,
hear a piercing siren, and are in love
with the inexplicable. You walk

to your car, find the hazard lights
blinking: find a rust-brown knife, a trout,
a smashed violin in your hands.
And then you wake, inside the dream,

to find tangerines ripening in the silence.
You peel the leaves of the dream
as you would peel the leaves off an onion.
The layers of the dream have no core,

no essence. You find a tattoo of
a red scorpion on your body.
You simply laugh, shiver in the frost,
and step back into the world.

2 A Galápagos turtle has nothing to do
with the world of the neutrino.
The ecology of the Galápagos Islands
has nothing to do with a pair of scissors.
The cactus by the window has nothing to do
with the invention of the wheel.
The invention of the telescope
has nothing to do with a red jaguar.
No. The invention of the scissors
has everything to do with the invention of the telescope.
A map of the world has everything to do
with the cactus by the window.
The world of the quark has everything to do
with a jaguar circling in the night.
The man who sacrifices himself and throws a Molotov
cocktail at a tank has everything to do
with a sunflower that bends to the light.

3 Open a window and touch the sun,
or feel the wet maple leaves flicker in the rain.
Watch a blue crab scuttle in clear water,
or find a starfish in the dirt.
Describe the color green to the colorblind,
or build a house out of pain.

The world is more than you surmise.
Take the pines, green-black, slashed by light,
etched by wind, on the island
across the riptide body of water.
Describe the thousand iridescent needles
to a blind albino Tarahumara.

In a bubble chamber, in a magnetic field,
an electron spirals and spirals in to the center,
but the world is more than such a dance:
a spiraling in to the point of origin,
a spiraling out in the form of a
wet leaf, a blue crab, or a green house.

4 The heat ripples ripple the cactus.
Crushed green glass in a parking lot
or a pile of rhinoceros bones
give off heat, though you might not notice it.

The heat of a star can be measured
under a spectrometer, but not
the heat of the mind, or the heat of Angkor Wat.
And the rubble of Angkor Wat

gives off heat; so do apricot blossoms
in the night, green fish, black bamboo,
or a fisherman fishing in the snow.
And an angstrom of shift turns the pleasure

into pain. The ice that rips the fingerprint
off your hand gives off heat;
and so does each moment of existence.
A red red leaf, disintegrating in the dirt,

burns with the heat of an acetylene flame.
And the heat rippling off
the tin roof of the adobe house
is simply the heat you see.

5

What is the secret to a Guarneri violin?
Wool dipped in an indigo bath turns bluer
when it oxidizes in the air. Marat is
changed in the minds of the living.
A shot of tequila is related to Antarctica
shrinking. A crow in a bar or red snapper on ice
is related to the twelve-tone method
of composition. And what does the tuning of tympani
have to do with the smell of your hair?
To feel, at thirty, you have come this far –
to see a bell over a door as a bell
over a door, to feel the care and precision
of this violin is no mistake, nor is the
sincerity and shudder of passion by which you live.

6 Crush an apple, crush a possibility.
No single method can describe the world;
therein is the pleasure
of chaos, of leaps in the mind.
A man slumped over a desk in an attorney's office
is a parrot fish caught in a seaweed mass.
A man who turns to the conversation in a bar
is a bluefish hooked on a cigarette.
Is the desire and collapse of desire in an unemployed carpenter
the instinct of salmon to leap upstream?
The smell of eucalyptus can be incorporated
into a theory of aggression.
The pattern of interference in a hologram
replicates the apple, knife, horsetails on the table,
but misses the sense of chaos, distorts
in its singular view. Then
touch, shine, dance, sing, be, becoming, be.

THE APHRODISIAC

"Power is my aphrodisiac."
Power enables him to
connect a candle-lit dinner
to the landing on the moon.
He sees a plot in the acid
content of American soil,
malice in the configuration
of palm-leaf shadows.
He is obsessed with
the appearance of democracy
in a terrorized nation.
If the price of oil
is an owl claw, a nuclear
reactor is a rattlesnake
fang. He has no use
for the song of an oriole,
bright yellow wings.
He refuses to consider
a woman in a wheelchair
touching the shadow of
a sparrow, a campesino
dreaming of spring.
He revels in the instant
before a grenade explodes.

THE ANSEL ADAMS CARD

You left a trail of bad checks in forty-six states.
When you were finally arrested on a check for $36.10,
you no longer knew how many aliases you had burned
out. You simply knew you had waited too long at the checkout
counter. The police found five sets of current driver's
licenses in your car, titles to ten other cars,
two diamond rings, and $2500 cash.

You started by running off with an ex-convict,
forging your mother's signature at the post office,
collecting her mail, and cashing a check.
You bought a car and groceries with the check:
took off, then, to Chicago. The scenario
was to open a checking account for fifty dollars,
withdraw forty at the end of the day, and use the blank
checks to shop with. Again and again: how many
times until you saw your signature at the checkout counter?
Once, you thought quickly, pulled out a license
with a different name, ran out to your husband
waiting in the car.

And he was scot-free: a tattoo of white lightning
on his arms. Now he is a used car salesman in Kansas City –
forging car titles and duplicating sales?
I see you as a green leaf in sunshine
after a rain. If you are paroled in July,
what will happen? Surely you won't forget life in prison,
jumping bail, on the run, the rape, the humiliation,
the arrest? But you are walking on glass.

You are now married to an inmate in Texarkana.
I give you this Ansel Adams card with one aspen, leafy,
against a forest, one aspen bright in the sun.

NEW WAVE

He listens to a punk rock group,
Dead on Arrival,
on his miniature Sony headphones and cassette recorder.
With the volume turned up,
the noise of the world
can't touch him.
No one's going to tell *him* what to do:
whether to drive
his car up an arroyo,
or wire the house with explosives.
He's given us the rap
on New Wave:
how it's noise and is disgusting –
though we suspect
whatever he dislikes is New Wave.
His mind is a Geiger counter bombarded with radiation:
the clusters of
click click click click, click click
a daily dose of carcinogens
without which
it would be impossible to live.
He watches us listen to a Jewish astrologer
reading a horoscope,
and glances out the window.
Now he flips
the cassette and turns up the volume.
I can see the headlines now:
Juvenile Detonates House,
pleads temporary insanity
due to the effects of listening to Agent Orange.

EVERY WHERE AND EVERY WHEN

1 Catch a moth in the Amazon; pin it under glass.
See the green-swirling magenta-flecked wings

miming a fierce face. And dead, watch it fly.
Throw a piece of juniper into a fire.

Search out the Odeon in Zurich to find Lenin or Klee.
No one has a doctrine of recollection to

bring back knowledge of what was, is?
The Odeon café is not the place to look

for Lenin's fingerprint. The piece of burning juniper
has the sound of the bones of your hands

breaking. And the moth at the window, magenta-flecked,
green-swirling, is every where and every when.

2 Everything is supposed to fit: mortise and tenon,
arteries and veins, hammer, anvil, stirrup in the ear,

but it does not fit. Someone was executed
today. Tomorrow friends of the executed will execute

the executers. And this despair is the intensifying
fever and chill, in shortening intervals,

of a malaria patient. Evil is not a variety of
potato found in the Andes. The smell of a gardenia

is not scissors and sponge in the hands of
an inept surgeon. Everything is supposed to fit:

but wander through Cuzco and the orientation of
streets and plazas is too Spanish. Throw

hibiscus on a corpse. Take an aerial view;
see the city built in the shape of a jaguar's head.

3 I pick a few mushrooms in the hills,
but do not know the lethal from the edible.

I cannot distinguish red wood dyed
with cochineal or lac, but know that

cochineal with alum, tin, salt, and lime juice
makes a rosé, a red, a burgundy.

Is it true an antimatter particle
never travels as slowly as the speed of light,

and, colliding with matter, explodes?
The mind shifts as the world shifts.

I look out the window, watch Antares glow.
The world shifts as the mind shifts;

or this belief, at least, increases
the pleasure of it all – the smell of espresso

in the street, picking blueberries,
white-glazed, blue-black,

sieved gold from a river, this moment
when we spin and shine.

THE REHEARSAL

Xylophone, triangle, marimba, soprano, violin –
the musicians use stopwatches, map out
in sound the convergence of three rivers at a farm,

but it sounds like the jungle at midnight.
Caught in a blizzard and surrounded by wolves
circling closer and closer, you might

remember the smell of huisache on a warm spring night.
You might remember three deer startled and stopped
at the edge of a road in a black canyon.

A child wants to act crazy, acts crazy,
is thereby sane. If you ache with longing
or are terrified: ache, be terrified, be hysterical,

walk into a redwood forest and listen:
hear a pine cone drop into a pool of water.
And what is your life then? In the time

it takes to make a fist or open your hand,
the musicians have stopped. But a life only stops
when what you want is no longer possible.

KAYAKING AT NIGHT ON TOMALES BAY

Kayak on the black water,
and feel a gold feather float in the air.
Pick up a red shard in the dirt,
and feel someone light a
candle and sing.

A man may die crashing into a redwood house,
or die as someone pries
open an oyster.
A kayaker may hit a rock, and
drown at the bottom of a waterfall.

Is the world of the dead
a world of memory? Or a world of ten dimensions?
Calculate the number of
configurations to a tangram?
Compute the digits of pi?

Kayak on the black water,
and feel the moonlight glisten the pines.
Drift, drift, and drifting:
the lights of cars on the road take a
thousand years to arrive.

MISTAKING WATER HEMLOCK FOR PARSLEY

Mistaking water hemlock for parsley,
I die two hours
later in the hospital;
or I turn the shish kebab on the hibachi,
and reel, crash
to the floor, die of a ruptured aorta.

Then you place an ear of blue corn
in my left hand,
tie a single turkey feather
around my right ankle.
I hear the coffin nailed shut,
hear green singing finches in the silence.

And in the silence I float on water,
feel an equilibrium,
feel the gravitational pull of the universe
slow everything down
and begin to draw everything back
to the center.

Then a star is a taste of olives,
a sun the shine on the black wings of ravens.
I wake, and joy and love, and feel
each passion makes me,
protean, wiser, stronger.
I want to live and live and live and live.

EVIL GRIGRI

Evil grigri:
taste acid in the word *sybaritic*.
Feel deer antlers polished in rain and sun;
taste green almonds,
the polar icecap of Mars melting at the tip of your tongue.

Is it possible to wake
dressed in a tuxedo smoking a cigarette staring at a firing
squad?
A man is cursed
when he remembers he cannot remember his dream;
taste sugar in the word *voluptuous*;
feel a macaw feather brush across your closed eyelids.

See the dead laugh at the pile of shoes at Dachau.
See as a man with one eye
the dead alive and singing,
walking down the equinoctial axis of the midnight street.

Now feel how the ocarina of your body
waits for pleasure to blow and make an emerald sound in the
air;
make an apotropaic prayer
that the day's evil become the day's wild thyme:

say guava-passionflower-hibiscus salt,
say sun-sea wave,
say wind-star, venom-night,
say mango-river, eucalpytus-scented fang.

THE PULSE

A woman in a psychiatric ward
is hysterical; she has to get a letter
to God by tomorrow or

the world will end. Which root
of a chiasma grows and grows?
Which dies? An analysis of

the visual cortex of the brain
confines your worldview even as you
try to enlarge it? I walk

down an arroyo lined with old tires
and broken glass, feel a pulse,
a rhythm in silence, a slow

blooming of leaves. I know
it is unlikely, but feel I could
find the bones of a whale

as easily as a tire iron.
I shut my eyes, green water flowing
in the acequia never returns.

THE DIAMOND POINT

Use the diamond point of grief:
incise a clear hibiscus in the windowpane.
A child picks apples in autumn light;
five minutes resemble a day?
But an aquamarine instant dropped
into water makes an entire pool shine.
Do you feel the forsythia about to explode?
The flow in a dead seal washed to shore?
I see the sloping street
to your house, bird of paradise in bloom:

silence when you lift the receiver off the phone,
shaft of spring light when you say, "Hello."
I see you smile in a flower dress –
intense pain, intense joy – waving goodbye,
goodbye, goodbye, goodbye, goodbye
1947, 1960, 1967, 1972, 1981.
A firework explodes in a purple chrysanthemum:
ooh and aah and then, then
use the diamond point of grief:
incise a clear hibiscus in the windowpane.

METASTASIS

Noon summer solstice light shines on a creation spiral
petroglyph.
We stare up at a pictograph of a left hand,
a new moon, a supernova of 1054 AD.
I dream of touching a rattlesnake,
want to find a fossil
of a green ginkgo leaf here in Chaco Wash.
I have not forgotten the death of Josephine Miles,
but forget grief,
that fried tripe;
I want to hike the thousand summer trails,
become sun, moon.
A rattlesnake slides into a coil:
if grief, grief, if pain, pain, if joy, joy.
In a night rain
all the emotions of a day become pure and shining.
I think, I no longer think:
metastasis: noon summer solstice light: turpentine, rags:
the new leaves of a peach delicate
and of light-green hue.

HORSE FACE

A man in prison is called horse face, but does nothing
when everyone in the tailor shop has sharp cold scissors;

he remembers the insult but laughs it off. Even as he
laughs, a Cattaraugus Indian welding a steel girder

turns at a yell which coincides with the laugh and slips
to his death. I open a beer, a car approaches a garage.

The door opens, a light comes on, inside rakes gleam;
a child with dysentery washes his hands in cow piss.

I find a trail of sawdust, walk in a dead killer's
hardened old shoes, and feel how difficult it is to

sense the entire danger of a moment: a horse gives birth
to a foal, power goes out in the city, a dancer

stops in the dark and listening for the noise that was scored
in the performance hears only sudden panicked yells.

THE NEGATIVE

A man hauling coal in the street is stilled forever.
Inside a temple, instead of light

a slow shutter lets the darkness in.
I see a rat turn a corner running from a man with a chair trying
to smash it,

see people sleeping at midnight in a Wuhan street on bamboo
beds,
a dead pig floating, bloated, on water.

I see a photograph of a son smiling who two years ago fell off a
cliff
and his photograph is in each room of the apartment.

I meet a woman who had smallpox as a child, was abandoned
by her mother
but who lived, now has two daughters, a son, a son-in-law;

they live in three rooms and watch a color television.
I see a man in blue work clothes whose father was a peasant

who joined the Communist party early but by the time of the
Cultural Revolution
had risen in rank and become a target of the Red Guards.

I see a woman who tried to kill herself with an acupuncture
needle
but instead hit a vital point and cured her chronic asthma.

A Chinese poet argues that the fundamental difference between
East and West
is that in the East an individual does not believe himself

in control of his fate but yields to it.
As a negative reverses light and dark

these words are prose accounts of personal tragedy becoming
metaphor,
an emulsion of silver salts sensitive to light,

laughter in the underground bomb shelter converted into a
movie theater,
lovers in the Summer Palace park.

WASABI

Quinine is to cinchona
as pain is to nerves? No,
as the depletion of ozone is to a city? No,

like a DNA double helix,
the purity of intention
is linked to the botched attempt.

The zing of a circular saw
is linked in time to
the smell of splintery charred plywood dust.

And the scent of red ginger
to a field guide is as
a blueprint to walking out of sunlight

into a cool stone Lama temple?
The mind at chess,
the mind at go: here

the purpose is not to prevail,
but to taste – as ikebana
is to spring cherry blossoms – wasabi.

THE SOLDERER

I watch a man soldering positive and negative speaker
wires to a plug inhale tin-lead alloy smoke.

He does not worry about a shift in the solar wind.
He does not worry about carcinogens.

Are his mind and memory as precise as his hands?
To suffer and suffer is not a necessary and sufficient

condition for revelation; open up a box of
Balinese flowers, roots, bark: the history of civilization

is to know you do not know what to do.
In my mind I practice rubbing a bronze spouting bowl

with both hands. The bowl begins to hum
and a standing wave makes the water splash up into my face.

I am stunned to hear a man who wore a T-shirt
with a silk-screened tie shot himself and is in critical

condition in the hospital. No one wants to
die suspended in air like gold dust flecked by sunlight.

RENGA

We hunger for the iridescent shine of an abalone shell

Stare at a newspaper, see the latest terrors

Want the sound of hail on a tin roof to reverberate forever

Want to feel the echo as we wash a rag, pick broccoli, sneeze

The sound does not make us forget the terrors

But the terrors are lived then as water in a stream

We hold, as in a tea ceremony, a bowl with both hands

Turn it a quarter-turn, and another, and another

And when we see the green stillness

See the abalone shine, abalone shine

TEN THOUSAND TO ONE

The Phoenicians guarded a recipe that required
ten thousand murex shells to make
an ounce of Tyrian purple.

Scan the surface of Aldebaran with a radio wave;
grind lapis lazuli
into ultramarine.

Search the summer sky for an Anasazi turkey constellation;
see algae under an electron microscope
resemble a Magellanic Cloud.

A chemist tried to convert benzene into quinine,
but blundered into a violet
aniline dye instead.

Have you ever seen maggots feed on a dead rat?
Listen to a red-tailed hawk glide
over the hushed spruce and

pines in a canyon. Feel a drop of water roll
down a pine needle, and glisten,
hanging, at the tip.

TO A COMPOSER

Red chair, blue chair, white chair, big chair, chair.
No, this is not the taste
of unripe persimmons,
nor standing on a New York street in December inhaling shish
  kebab smoke.
The dissonant sounds played on a piano
become macaws perched on cages.
A green Amazon parrot with yellow-tipped wings
lands on your shoulder.
The background hum
of loudspeakers becomes a humid environment.
You may open this door and walk into the aviary
when you least expect to,
startled walk on redwood planks over huge-leafed tropical
  plants
as a red-billed toucan flaps by.
Dirty utensils are piled in the sink,
coffee grinds clog the drain.
So what if the plumber pouring sulfuric acid
gives you a look
when you open the refrigerator
and pull out a just solidified chocolate turkey in a pan?
This is not 5:14 sharpening a pencil
but inhaling deeply and feeling the stream of air poured out
  through a *shakuhachi*
become a style of living.

SHOOTING STAR

1 In a concussion,
the mind severs the pain:
you don't remember flying off a motorcycle,
and landing face first
in a cholla.

But a woman stabbed in her apartment,
by a prowler searching for
money and drugs,
will never forget her startled shriek
die in her throat,
blood soaking into the floor.

The quotidian violence of the world
is like a full moon rising over the Ortiz mountains;
its pull is everywhere.
But let me live a life of violent surprise
and startled joy. I want to
thrust a purple iris into your hand,
give you a sudden embrace.

I want to live as Wang Hsi-chih lived
writing characters in gold ink on black silk –
not to frame on a wall,
but to live the splendor now.

2 Deprived of sleep, she hallucinated
and, believing she had sold the genetic
research on carp, signed a confession.
Picking psilocybin mushrooms in the mountains

of Veracruz, I hear tin cowbells
in the slow rain, see men wasted on pulque
sitting under palm trees. Is it
so hard to see things as they truly are:

a route marked in red ink on a map,
the shadows of apricot leaves thrown
in wind and sun on a wall? It is
easy to imagine a desert full of agaves

and golden barrel cactus, red earth, a red sun.
But to truly live one must see things
as they are, as they might become:
a wrench is not a fingerprint

on a stolen car, nor baling wire
the undertow of the ocean. I may hallucinate,
but see the men in drenched clothes
as men who saw and saw and refuse to see.

3 Think of being a judge or architect
or trombonist, and do not worry whether
thinking so makes it so. I overhear
two men talking in another room;

I cannot transcribe the conversation
word for word, but know if they are
vexed or depressed, joyful or nostalgic.
An elm leaf floats on a pond.

Look, a child wants to be a cardiologist
then a cartographer, but wanting so
does not make it so. It is not
a question of copying out the Heart Sutra

in your own blood on an alabaster wall.
It is not a question of grief or joy.
But as a fetus grows and grows,
as the autumn moon ripens the grapes,

greed and cruelty and hunger for power
ripen us, enable us to grieve, act,
laugh, shriek, see, see it all as
the water on which the elm leaf floats.

4 Write out the memories of your life
in red-gold disappearing ink, so that it all
dies, no lives. Each word you speak
dies, no lives. Is it all
at once in the mind? I once stepped
on a sea urchin, used a needle to dig out
the purple spines; blood soaked my hands.
But one spine was left, and I carried
it a thousand miles. I saw then
the olive leaves die on the branch,
saw dogs tear flesh off a sheep's corpse.
To live at all is to grieve;
but, once, to have it all at once
is to see a shooting star: shooting star
shooting star.

THE SILENCE

We walk through a yellow-ocher adobe house:
the windows are smeared with grease,
the doors are missing. Rain leaks
through the ceilings of all the rooms,
and the ribs of saguaro thrown across *vigas*
are dark, wet, and smell. The view outside
of red-faded and turquoise-faded adobes
could be Chihuahua, but it isn't.
I stop and look through an open doorway,
see wet newspapers rotting in mud
in the small center patio.
I suddenly see red bougainvillea blooming
against a fresh whitewashed wall,
smell yellow wisteria through an open
window on a warm summer night;
but, no, a shot of cortisone is no cure
for a detaching retina. I might just
as well see a smashed dog in the street,
a boojum tree pushing its way up
through asphalt. And as we turn
and arrive where we began, I notice
the construction of the house is
simply room after room forming a square.
We step outside, and the silence is as
water is, taking the shape of the container.

KEOKEA

Black wattles along the edge of the clearing
below the house: a few koa plants are fenced in.

An old horse nibbles grass near the loquat tree.
Sunburned from hiking twelve miles into a volcano,

I do not know what I am looking at. Koa?
I want to walk into an empty charred house

and taste a jacaranda blossom.
Here Sun Yat-sen pounded his fist, sold opium,

dreamed the Chinese Revolution until blood broke
inside his brain? Marvin Miura is running

for political office; he wants aquaculture
for Maui, a ti leaf wrapped around a black river

stone, and he may get it. But one needs
to walk into a charred house where the sensuous

images of the world can be transformed. Otherwise
we can sit up all night on the redwood decking,

argue greed and corruption, the price of sugar cane,
how many pearls Imelda Marcos owns.

EARLY AUTUMN

I almost squashed a tarantula on the road.
And once when I found
earthstars growing under pines

almost sliced one open
but stopped.
The Mayans keyed their lives to the motion of Venus

but timing is human not Hegelian.
A revolutionary never waits
for cities to arrive

at appropriate orthodox Marxist conditions
to act.
A man used a chain saw

to cut yellow cedar,
but when he finished
discovered a minus tide had beached his skiff.

I've lived 12,680 days
and dreamed gold plankton flashing in my hands.
It flashes now

as I watch
red dragonflies vanish over water.
A blue tarantula crossed highway 286.

NOTHING CAN HEAL THE SEVERED NERVES OF A HAND?

Nothing can heal the severed nerves of a hand?
No one can stop feeling the touch of things
as the nerves die? A wasp lands on a yellow
but still green-veined leaf floating on water –
two dead flies drift aside. An old man
draws a llama on roller skates, remembers
arguing cases in court, now argues in a wheelchair
with whoever arrives. The nurses hate him,
but forget a life lived without mallet and chisel
is lived without scars. Then think how long
it takes the body to heal, the mind to shine.
An acupuncturist pushes a needle into your ear:
you incandesce. Yes. Yes, more, all, no, less, none.
Prune the branches of a pear at midnight;
taste a pine needle on a branch without touching it;
feel a seed germinate in the dark, sending
down roots, sending up leaves, ah!

SPLASH, FLOW

The unerring tragedy of our lives is to sail
a papyrus sailboat across the Atlantic ocean,

discover corn fossils in China: splash, flow.
When the bones of a platypus are found at Third Mesa,

the *Kooyemsi* will laugh. Watch a papyrus sailboat
slowly sink into the Mediterranean;

feel how grief, like a mordant, quietly attaches
pain to your nerves. *Now* splash, flow:

taste the sunrise shining inside your hands,
be jalapeño, wine, salt, gold, fire;

rejoice as your child finds a Malodorous Lepiota
under myrtle, smell the sea at night

as you hold the woman you love in your arms.

THE MOMENT OF CREATION

A painter indicates the time of day
in a still life: afternoon light slants on a knife,
lemons, green wine bottle with some red wine.
We always leave something unfinished?
We want x and having x want y and having y want z?
I try to sense the moment of creation
in the shine on a sliced lemon. I want to
connect throwing gravel on mud to being hungry.
"Eat," a man from Afghanistan said
and pointed to old rotting apples in the opened car trunk.
I see a line of men dancing a cloud dance;
two women dance intricate lightning steps
at either end. My mistakes and failures
pulse in me even as moments of joy,
but I want the bright moments to resonate out
like a gamelan gong. I want to make
the intricate tessellated moments of our lives
a floor of jade, obsidian, turquoise, ebony, lapis.

FORGET FEZ

Algol, Mizar:
I wanted to become pure like the Arabic
names of stars,

but perhaps I have erred.
At sunrise

the song of an ordinary robin startles me.
I want to say vireo,

but it *is* a robin.
In bed I turn and breathe
with your breath,

remember four days ago opening my hands
to a man who blessed me

and others with an eagle feather.
Betelgeuse, Deneb:

moonshine on a clear summer night,
but the splendor
is to taste smoke in your hair.

Forget Fez.

SHUTTLE

She is making stuffing for the turkey;
a few pistachio shells are on the kitchen table.
He looks out the window at the thermometer,

but sees a winter melon with a white glaze
in a New York Chinatown store at night.
Large sea bass swim in a tank by the window;

there are delicate blue crabs in a can
climbing and climbing on each other to get out.
She is thinking of a tapestry of red horses

running across a Southwestern landscape
with blue mesas in the distance. A shuttle goes
back and forth, back and forth through

the different sheds. He is talking to a man
who photographs empty parks in New York,
sees the branches of a black magnolia in early December.

She is washing out yarn so it will pack
and cover the warp; perhaps the tension
isn't right; the texture of Churro fleece

makes her hands tingle; a pot of walnuts
boils on the stove. He turns on the radio,
and listening to Nigerian music

feels the rumble of a subway under the floor,
feels the warmth of his hands
as he watches the snow fall and fall.

THROWING SALT ON A PATH

I watch you throw salt on the path,
and see abalone divers point to the sun,
discuss the waves, then throw their

gear back into the car. I watch you
collect large flakes of salt off rocks,
smell sliced ginger and fresh red

shrimp smoking over a fire. Ah,
the light of a star never stops, but travels
at the expanding edge of the universe.

A Swiss gold watch ticks and ticks;
but when you cannot hear it tick anymore,
it turns transparent in your hand.

You see the clear gold wheels
with sharp minute teeth catching each
other and making each spin.

The salt now clears a path in the snow,
expands the edges of the universe.

EDNA BAY

One day the men pulled a house off float logs
up on land with a five-ton winch and a system of pulleys,
while a woman with a broken tooth chewed aspirin

and watched. A man was cutting down a red cedar
with a chain saw when it kicked back in his face,
cut his chin and hand to bone. A neighbor called Ketchikan

through a marine operator and chartered a plane
out before dark. Life on Kosciusko Island
is run by the weather and tides. Is the rain today

from the southeast or southwest? If southeast,
the men go into the rain forest cursing:
it will be hard to dig out pilings for a house.

I see how these fishermen hate seiners and humpies,
want to spend days and days trolling at twenty-four fathoms.
I watch a great blue heron knife herring at low tide,

see a bald eagle circle and circle the shoreline.
One night with the full moon and a wind
on my face, I went across the bay in a skiff

looking at the rippling black water.
Days I will wake startled dreaming of bear,
see sheets of thin ice floating out in the bay.

BLACK JAVA PEPPER

Despair, anger, grief:
as a seiner indiscriminately hauls
humpies, jellyfish, kelp,
we must – farouche,

recalcitrant – conversely
angle for sockeye.
Our civilization has no genetic code
to make wasps return

each spring to build a nest
by the water heater
in the shed. We must – igneous,
metamorphic – despite

such plans as to push Mt. Fuji into the ocean
to provide more land –
grind cracked black
Java pepper into our speech

so that – limestone into marble,
granite into gneiss –
we become through our griefs –
rain forest islands – song.

THE HALIBUT

Dipping spruce branches into the calm water
to collect herring eggs
is an azure unthinking moment.
A fisherman never forgets the violet hue of December stars.
Does time make memory or memory make time
    polychromatic?
Squawk.
In a split second one hears a Steller's jay, raven,
car tires on gravel, chain saw, fly, wind chime.
This constellation of polychromatic sounds
becomes a crimson moment
that, fugitive-colored, will fade.
But one never forgets lighting kerosene lamps before noon.
In July when one has twenty hours of light
each second is fuchsia dyed.
One might be pouring Clorox down a hose to flush out an
    octopus
when one feels the moment explode,
when a fisherman using power crank and long line
looks into the water and sees
rising a two-hundred-pound halibut with bulging eyes.

STANDING ON AN ALDER BRIDGE OVER A CREEK

At low tide, midnight, with a flashlight,
we walk along the shore stumbling
on rocks, slightly drunk, step

through a creek where arctic water pours in
over my boots; nothing to do but
go on. We come to a tidal pool,

stop, see the exposed colonies of blue-black
mussels, go up to a trail, come
to an alder bridge; stop:

let the mature mind consider danger,
guess the architecture of a Persian house
in a dream contains the sockeye

an osprey hungers for. If so,
then emerald *if*: no, despair?
Like the camouflage of snowy plover eggs

in sand and bright sunshine,
we stand on an alder bridge over a creek,
are the April starlight and laugh.

HERE

Here a snail on a wet leaf shivers and dreams of spring.
Here a green iris in December.
Here the topaz light of the sky.
Here one stops hearing a twig break and listens for deer.
Here the art of the ventriloquist.
Here the obsession of a kleptomaniac to steal red pushpins.
Here the art of the alibi.
Here one walks into an abandoned farmhouse and hears a
 tarantella.
Here one dreamed a bear claw and died.
Here a humpback whale leaped out of the ocean.
Here the outboard motor stopped but a man made it to this
 island with one oar.
Here the actor forgot his lines and wept.
Here the art of prayer.
Here marbles, buttons, thimbles, dice, pins, stamps, beads.
Here one becomes terrified.
Here one wants to see as a god sees and becomes clear amber.
Here one is clear pine.

PARALLAX

"Kwakwha."
"Askwali."
The shift in Hopi when a man or woman says "thank you"
becomes a form of parallax.
A man travels

from Mindanao to Kyushu and says his inner geography
is enlarged by each new place.
Is it?
Might he not grow more by staring for twenty-four hours
at a single pine needle?

I watch a woman tip an ashtray and empty
a few ashes into her mouth,
but ah, I want
other soliloquies.
I want equivalents to Chu-ko Liang sending his fire ships

downstream into Ts'ao Ts'ao's fleet.
It does not mean
a geneticist must quit
and devote his life to the preservation of rhinoceros,
but it might mean

watching a thousand snow geese drift on water
as the sky darkens minute by minute.
"Kwakwha,"
"Askwali,"
whenever, wherever.

THE DAY CAN BECOME A ZEN GARDEN OF RAKED SAND

The day can become a Zen garden of raked sand
or a yellow tanager singing on a branch;

feel the terrors and pleasures of the morning:
in Tianjin all the foreigners are sent to a movie

and they must guess at what the authorities
do not wish them to see; dream a rainy landscape:

the Jemez Mountains breaking up in mist and jagged light
into a series of smaller but dazzling ranges;

to distinguish the smell of calendula from delphinium
is of no apparent consequence, but guess that

crucial moments in history involve an unobtrusive
point flaring into a startling revelation;

now be alive to the flowering chives by the window;
feel the potato plant in the whiskey barrel soak up sun;

feel this riparian light,
this flow where no word no water is.

THE UNNAMABLE RIVER

1 Is it in the anthracite face of a coal miner,
crystalized in the veins and lungs of a steel
worker, pulverized in the grimy hands of a railroad engineer?
Is it in a child naming a star, coconuts washing
ashore, dormant in a volcano along the Rio Grande?

You can travel the four thousand miles of the Nile
to its source and never find it.
You can climb the five highest peaks of the Himalayas
and never recognize it.
You can gaze through the largest telescope
and never see it.

But it's in the capillaries of your lungs.
It's in the space as you slice open a lemon.
It's in a corpse burning on the Ganges,
in rain splashing on banana leaves.

Perhaps you have to know you are about to die
to hunger for it. Perhaps you have to go
alone into the jungle armed with a spear
to truly see it. Perhaps you have to
have pneumonia to sense its crush.

But it's also in the scissor hands of a clock.
It's in the precessing motion of a top
when a torque makes the axis of rotation describe a cone:
and the cone spinning on a point gathers
past, present, future.

2 In a crude theory of perception, the apple you
see is supposed to be a copy of the actual apple,
but who can step out of his body to compare the two?
Who can step out of his life and feel
the Milky Way flow out of his hands?

An unpicked apple dies on a branch;
that is all we know of it.
It turns black and hard, a corpse on the Ganges.
Then go ahead and map out three thousand miles of the Yangtze;
walk each inch, feel its surge and
flow as you feel the surge and flow in your own body.

And the spinning cone of a precessing top
is a form of existence that gathers and spins death and life into one.
It is in the duration of words, but beyond words –
river river river, river river.
The coal miner may not know he has it.
The steel worker may not know he has it.
The railroad engineer may not know he has it.
But it is there. It is in the smell
of an avocado blossom, and in the true passion of a kiss.

ARCHIPELAGO (1995)

STREAMERS

1 As an archaeologist unearths a mask with opercular teeth
and abalone eyes, someone throws a broken fan and extension cords
into a dumpster. A point of coincidence exists in the mind

resembling the tension between a denotation and its stretch
of definition: aurora: a luminous phenomenon consisting
of streamers or arches of light appearing in the upper atmosphere

of a planet's polar regions, caused by the emission of light
from atoms excited by electrons accelerated along the planet's
magnetic field lines. The mind's magnetic field lines.

When the red shimmering in the huge dome of sky stops,
a violet flare is already arcing up and across, while a man
foraging a dumpster in Cleveland finds some celery and charred fat.

Hunger, angst: the blue shimmer of emotion, water speeding
through a canyon; to see only to know: to wake finding
a lug nut, ticket stub, string, personal card, ink smear, $2.76.

2 A Kwakiutl wooden dish with a double-headed wolf
is missing from a museum collection. And as

the director checks to see if it was deaccessioned,
a man sitting on a stool under bright lights

shouts: a pachinko ball dropped vertiginously
but struck a chiming ring and ricocheted to the left.

We had no sense that a peony was opening,
that a thousand white buds of a Kyoto camellia

had opened at dusk and had closed at dawn.
When the man steps out of the pachinko parlor,

he will find himself vertiginously dropping
in starless space. When he discovers

that his daughter was cooking over smoking oil
and shrieked in a fatal asthma attack,

he will walk the bright streets in an implosion of grief,
his mind will become an imploding star,

he will know he is searching among bright gold threads
for a black pattern in the weave.

3 Set a string loop into a figure of two diamonds,
four diamonds, one diamond:
as a woman tightens her hand into a fist
and rubs it in a circular motion over her heart,
a bewildered man considering the semantics of *set*
decides no through-line exists:

to sink the head of a nail below the surface,
to fix as a distinguishing imprint, sign, or appearance,
to incite, put on a fine edge by grinding,
to adjust, adorn, put in motion, make unyielding,
to bend slightly the tooth points of a saw
alternately in opposite directions.

As the woman using her index finger makes
spiral after spiral from her aorta up over her head,
see the possibilities for transcendence:
you have to die and die in your mind
before you can begin to see the empty spaces
the configuration of string defines.

4 A restorer examines the pieces of a tin chandelier,
and notices the breaks in the arms are along
old solder lines, and that cheap epoxy was used.

He will have to scrape off the epoxy, scrub some flux,
heat up the chandelier and use a proper solder.
A pair of rough-legged hawks are circling over a pasture;

one hawk cuts off the rabbit's path of retreat
while the other swoops with sharp angle and curve of wings.
Cirrus, cirrostratus, cirrocumulus, altostratus,

altocumulus, stratocumulus, nimbostratus,
cumulus, cumulonimbus, stratus: is there no end?
Memories stored in the body begin to glow.

A woman seals basil in brown bags and hangs them
from the ceiling. A dead sturgeon washes to shore.
The sun is at the horizon, but another sun

is rippling in water. It's not that the angle
of reflection equals the angle of incidence,
but there's exultation, pleasure, distress, death, love.

5 The world resembles a cuttlefish changing colors
and shimmering. An apprentice archer has

stretched the bowstring properly, but does not know
he will miss the target because he is not aiming in the hips.

He will learn to hit the target without aiming
when he has died in his mind. I am not scared of death,

though I am appalled at how obsession with security
yields a pin-pushing, pencil-shaving existence.

You can descend to the swimming level of sharks,
be a giant kelp growing from the ocean bottom up

to the surface light, but the critical moment
is to die feeling the infinite stillness of the passions,

to revel in the touch of hips, hair, lips, hands,
feel the collapse of space in December light.

When I know I am no longer trying to know the spectral lines
of the earth, I can point to a cuttlefish and say,

"Here it is sepia," already it is deep-brown,
and exult, "Here it is deep-brown," already it is white.

6 Red koi swim toward us, and black
carp are rising out of the depths of the pond,
but our sustenance is a laugh, a grief,

a walk at night in the snow,
seeing the pure gold of a flickering candle –
a moment at dusk when we see

that deer have been staring at us,
we did not see them edge out of the brush,
a moment when someone turns on a light

and turns a window into a mirror,
a moment when a child asks,
"When will it be tomorrow?"

To say "A bell cannot be red and violet
at the same place and time because
of the logical structure of color" is true

but is a dot that must enlarge into
a zero: a void, *enso*, red shimmer,
breath, endless beginning, pure body, pure mind.

THE SILK ROAD

1 The blood in your arteries is contaminated with sugar.
You may hate the adrenal reduction of the mind to

the mind of a dog, but *sic*, *run* may be forms of sugar.
You may whet for the smell of rain on a clear summer night.

You may whet for the sugar in red maple leaves.
You may whet for the blue needle of a compass to point

north, and when it points north insist you wanted it
to point north-northwest. No, yes. In a dream

you catch a white turtle in a net and a voice says,
"Kill it, divine with it, and you shall have good luck,"

but discard dream structure for a deeper asymmetry.
You thirst in your mind for an insulin, death:

death in the yellow saguaro flower opening at midnight,
death in a canyon wren's song at sunrise,

death in red carp swimming in a clear pool of water,
death in an April moonrise. Now the figure-of-eight knot,

overhand knot, thief knot, loop knot, bowline knot,
slide knot, slipknot, sheepshank is pulled tighter and tighter.

2 You may stare out of a south window for hours
and feel the April sunlight dissolve the shifting leaves,

and you may dream sunlight opening a red camellia.
You may eat monkey brains and bear paws,

but, out of disordered passions and a disordered mind,
can you construct yellow doors that open in silence into summer?

You may repeat mistake after mistake so that you
will the mistakes into an accelerating spiral of despair.

A turtle pushes onto the sand of Bikini Island,
and, disoriented by radiation, pushes further and further

inland to die; but do not confuse the bones
of a cow bleached in the sun with disordered desire.

You may dream sunlight shining into a cool mountain forest
and wake up inhaling the smell of Douglas fir.

You may dream sea turtles swimming in black water
but wake sunstruck walking in shifting dunes of white sand.

Who can say *here, now* is metempsychosic delusion?
Can you set out for Turfan today and arrive yesterday at dusk?

3 A man in a hospital is waiting for a heart transplant.
He may fish at night under the stars with a cool salt wind;

he may soar out over the black shining waters of a bay.
He may want to die with sunlight shining on his face;

he may want to die in a tsunami, but his yes and his no
are a void. He may die as a gray squirrel cracks open an acorn;

he may die as a green terrapin slips into a stream.
As a diabetic shivers and sweats, shivers and sweats,

he feels the moonlight shining on the high tide waters of the bay.
He feels the drone of traffic slip into silence, and then

the trivial, the inconsequential stings him, stings him.
As a child, he said to his father, "That man is weird;

why does he wear a pillow under his pants?" And his father laughed,
"He's fat, so fat." Then, "The Chinese word for onion

is *cong*, so a green onion is *xiao cong*, small onion, yes?"
"Yes." "Then a large white onion must be *da cong*, large

onion, yes?" "No, a large white onion is called *yang cong*."
"*Yang cong*?" "Yes." "Which *yang*?" "The *yang* that means
ocean." "Shit."

4 The, a, this, the, tangerine, splash, hardly:
these threads of sound may be spun in s-spin into fiber:

lighted buoy, whistling buoy, spar buoy, bell buoy, buoy.
Hear the sounds of apricots dropping from branches to the earth;

feel the red vibration of wings before you see a hummingbird.
A man may travel from Mindanao to Macao to avoid

staring into himself; he may search at night in a helicopter
for the shimmer of a fire opal dropped into water;

he may inhale starlight as if it were a pungent yellow
flower opening slowly in the still August night.

To be still: watch a dog listen to sounds you cannot hear,
feel the pull of moonrise on the feathers of an owl.

There are apricots beginning to drop from branches to the earth;
there are apricots not yet beginning to drop from branches;

there are apricots not yet not yet beginning to drop.

5

This sand was black and silver shining in the megalight.
Now the radiation is in my hands and in your face.

You may dream red petals on a mountain path in rain;
I may watch the shimmer of light in the yellowing leaves.

Yes and no, spring and autumn have no power without the mind
that wills them into magnetic north, magnetic south.

A merchant from Xi'an brought ceremonial caps to Kuqa,
but the Kuqa people shaved their heads and tattooed their bodies.

To seal a dime in a red envelope and send it to
an insurance salesman is to send anthurium to a cannibal.

The taste of unripe persimmons, and pale moonlight shining
on the black hills appear to have no use: who

would have dreamed they would become, *shibui*, an aesthetic?
To argue that you must know the characteristic

that makes all birds birds before you can identify
a bird – and here you must discard antinomies –

postpones *auk* to that indeterminate time in the fallout
of the future when you shall have knowledge of the form *Death*.

6 Various proofs for the existence of God
try to predicate existence, but being

is unlike *yellow*, *sour*, *pungent*. That a branch
of the linden has yellow and dropping

leaves hardly enables us to infer that
water flowing through the underground *karez*

into Turfan is about to stop. If
the passions are the music of empty holes,

hear the blue and gold sounds of angst.
As I stared out the south window, I

saw the leaves of the linden green with no hint
of yellow. No, as I stared out the south

window, I wanted to see the yellowing leaves,
but instead saw, reflected in the glass

back through the space of the room
and out another window, salted skates

hanging on a wire to dry. So what I saw
reflected deflected my intention as now I say *now*.

OOLONG

1 Tea leaves wilted in sunlight are shaken
and bruised so that the edges redden
and veins turn transparent. A man at a counter
eats boiled silk worms and coughs;
a woman stops speaking and stares
at the constellation Perseus. Once,
a merchant smashed a black raku bowl
when it failed to please a tea master,
but, glued back together, the black shards
had the texture of mulberry leaves.
You pass someone bowing talking on the telephone,
and the shock is an incandescent quark
leaving a spiraling track in the mind:
you sense how, in a field guide, it is impossible
to know the growth arc of a mushroom,
but stumble upon shelves of oysters
growing out of dead aspens and
see how nothing in this world is yet yours.

2 True or false:

termites release methane and add to the greenhouse effect;

the skin of a blowfish is lethal;

crosses along roads in Mexico mark vehicular deaths;

the earth is flat;

oysters at full moon contain hepatitis;

no one has ever seen a neutrino;

butterflies dream;

the fins of a blowfish are always edible;

oolong means *black dragon*, but *oo* means *crow* and *long* means
  dragon;

he loved the curves of her body;

the sun revolves around the earth;

caffeine stimulates the central nervous system;

light is a wave;

the mind is composed of brightest bright and darkest dark;

context is crucial;

pfennigs, xu, qindarka, centimes, stotinki, qursh are coins;

the raw liver of a tiger blowfish
caught at winter solstice is a delicacy;

I have a knife inscribed with the names of forty-eight fish.

3 You sift curtains of red light
shimmering in the November sky,
sift the mind of a roofer mopping hot tar.
Walking down a hallway, you stop

and sift the brains in a glass bowl,
sift the tag dangling from the wrist of a corpse,
sift the folded wings of a sparrow.
The prevailing notions of the season

are green-stained lactarius prevailing
in the mountains for three days and an hour.
You have to reject ideas of disjunction
and collage, reject advice, praise.

Then you might look at a Song dynasty map
of Hangzhou and see the configuration
of ion channels in the brain. You might look
at an aboriginal sandpainting and see

a cosmology of grief. You might look
at the swaying motion of a branch
and feel what it is to be a
burned and shriveled leaf clinging to death.

4 I stare into a black bowl and smell
whisked green tea, see a flap of tails
and orange koi surging in a stream.
Sunlight is dropping down through tallest pines;
I stop on a bridge, and water
passes underneath and through me.
As a potter has a premonition of death
when he avoids using a red glaze on a square dish,
we come to know the form and pressure of an emotion
when it's gone: a soliloquy of despair
ends as a rope burn in the hands,
and pleasure flares into a gold chrysanthemum.
Is the spinning spinless when nothing is yours?
The mind slows to a green-flecked swirl;
I touch contours of the black shards.
Before sunrise, a man is cutting all
the morning glories blooming in the garden
and places one in a jar in a tearoom.

5

They smuggled his corpse into the city in a pile of rotting abalone;

"Very famous": they all nodded;

he knew the daphne was a forbidden flower;

"Twerp," a restaurant inspector muttered
and placed a C in the window;

they slurped noodles and read comic books;

he spits off the subway platform;

the slightest noise so disturbed him he had a soundproof room built:
white walls, white floor;

she kept feeling a snail on her neck;

for tea ceremony,
he cut three gentians and threw them into an Acoma pot;

she buried the placenta in the cornfield;

a hunter discovers a honey mushroom larger than a blue whale;

what opens and closes, closes and opens?

she took his breath away;

he dips his brush
and writes the character "flower" incorporating the character
"mind";

a flayed elephant skin;

she stir-fries tea leaves in a wok.

6 Red poppies are blooming along a wall;
I look at green and underlying blue paint
peeling off a bench: you rummage in a shed
and find a spindle, notice the oil of
hands has accumulated on the shaft.
In the rippling shadows, the shimmer of water.
I see yellow iris in a vase on the kitchen table
and smell lightning; commuters at the World
Trade Center may descend escalators to subways:
it is always 5:05; Su-wei brought him
five thousand yellow pills and said if
he swallowed twelve each day it would
restore his hair, but is this a form of
sipping sake steeped in a jar full of vipers?
Footprints under water in a rice paddy
and on the water's surface, clouds;
Altair and Vega spin in longing:
the sun dips below the horizon in a watery gold.

7 The mycelium of a honey mushroom
glows in the dark. What does a yellow
Man On Horseback know of winter and spring?
A farmer pushes his fist into clay

and forms a bowl. The world will continue
as long as two aborigines
clack boomerangs and chant?
A woman has the watery shine

of a sapphire and becomes yellow lightning.
She has a dream that resembles a geode:
if we could open it we might
recover the hue of the first world.

The light through a pressed octopus cup
has a rippling texture resembling
a cool undulating shadow over skin.
In the dark, the precession

and nutation of an emotion is a star:
Sirius, Arcturus, Capella, Procyon, Aldebaran:
shadows of mosquitoes are moving
along a rice-paper screen.

IN YOUR HONOR

In your honor, a man presents a sea bass
tied to a black-lacquered dish by green-spun seaweed.

"Ah" is heard throughout the room:
you are unsure what is about to happen.

You might look through a telescope at the full
bright moon against deep black space,

see from the Bay of Dew to the Sea of Nectar,
but, no, this beauty of naming is a subterfuge.

What are the thoughts of hunters driving
home on a Sunday afternoon empty-handed?

Their conception of honor may coincide
with your conception of cruelty? The slant

of light as sun declines is a knife
separating will and act into infinitely thin

and lucid slices. You look at the sea bass's eye,
clear and luminous. The gills appear to move

ever so slightly. The sea bass smells
of dream, but this is no dream. "Ah,

such delicacy" is heard throughout the room,
and the sea bass suddenly flaps. It

bleeds and flaps, bleeds and flaps as
the host slices slice after slice of glistening sashimi.

THE FLOWER PATH

Down to this north end of the verandah, across the view
of 1,001 gold-leafed statues of Kuan-yin looking west,
Wasa Daihachiro, in twenty-four hours in 1686, shot
13,054 arrows of which 8,133 were bull's eyes. Today
no one can pull the two hundred pound laminated bamboo bow
to send a single arrow with a low trajectory the length
of the thirty-three bays. As you walk on the verandah,
you see a tree full of white bags tied over peaches,
hear the sound of bells at a fish auction,
note the stares of men sitting on tiers under lights;
you are careful not to raise your hand as you examine
a two-hundred-pound tuna smoking just unpacked from dry ice;
at lunch you put a shrimp in your mouth and feel it twitch;
you enter a house and are dazed as your eyes adjust to
a hundred blind Darumas in the room;
you must learn to see a pond in the shape of the character "mind,"
walk through a garden and see it from your ankles;
a family living behind a flower-arrangement shop
presents the store as a face to the street;
the eldest daughter winces when the eighty-year-old parents
get out wedding pictures of the second daughter;
at night the belching sounds of frogs;
in the morning you look in rice paddies and find only tadpoles;
you are walking down into a gorge along the river,
turn to find stone piled on stone offerings along the path
and on rocks in midstream; in the depths of the cave,
a gold mirror with candles burning;
deer running at dusk in a dry moat;
iris blooming and about to bloom;
you are walking across Moon-Crossing Bridge in slashing rain,

meet a Rinzai monk with a fax machine
who likes to crank up a Victrola with a gold horn;
you see the red ocher upper walls of a teahouse,
and below the slatted bamboo fences called "dog repellers";
you stop at the south end of the verandah and look north;
an actor walks off the flower-path ramp cross-eyed amid shouts.

THE GREAT WHITE SHARK

For days he has dumped a trail of tuna blood
into the ocean so that a great white shark

might be lured, so that we might touch its fin.
The power of the primitive is parallactic:

in a museum exhibit, a *chacmool* appears as elegant
and sophisticated sculpture, as art, but

witness the priest rip the still-beating heart
out of the blue victim's body and place it

pulsing on a *chacmool* and we are ready to vomit.
We think the use of a beryllium gyroscope

marks technological superiority, but the urge
of ideologies then and now makes revenge inexorable.

The urge to skydive, rappel, white-water kayak
is the urge to release, the urge to die.

Diamond and graphite may be allotropic forms
of carbon, but what are the allotropic forms

of ritual and desire? The moon shining on black water,
yellow forsythia blossoming in the April night,

red maple leaves dropping in silence in October:
the seasons are not yet human forms of desire.

SLANTING LIGHT

Slanting light casts onto a stucco wall
the shadows of upwardly zigzagging plum branches.

I can see the thinning of branches to the very twig.
I have to sift what you say, what she thinks,

what he believes is genetic strength, what
they agree is inevitable. I have to sift this

quirky and lashing stillness of form to see myself,
even as I see laid out on a table for Death

an assortment of pomegranates and gourds.
And what if Death eats a few pomegranate seeds?

Does it insure a few years of pungent spring?
I see one gourd, yellow from midsection to top

and zucchini-green lower down, but
already the big orange gourd is gnawed black.

I have no idea why the one survives the killing nights.
I have to sift what you said, what I felt,

what you hoped, what I knew. I have to sift
death as the stark light sifts the branches of the plum.

RED OCTOPUS

She folds the four corners into the center,
hears the sound of a porcupine in a cornfield,
smells heart-shaped leaves in the dark.
She stops, noticing she has folded the red side out.
She is supposed to fold so that the red is seen
through white as what lies below surface.

So she restarts and folds the creases in air.
She recalls her mother arguing and flashing her party card;
she recalls soldiers at the Great Hall of the People
receive medals; she recalls her father film
a chimpanzee smoking a cigarette at the Beijing zoo;
she senses how the soldiers were betrayed.

She makes a petal fold, a valley fold,
an open-sink fold, a series of mountain folds,
pondering how truths were snared by malice.
She makes an inside-reverse fold, crimps the legs,
and, with a quick spurt of air,
inflates the body of the octopus.

WHITEOUT

You expect to see swirling chunks of ice
flowing south toward open water of the ocean,
but, no, a moment of whiteout as
the swirling ice flows north at sunset.
In a restaurant with an empty screen,
a woman gets up and sings a Chinese song
with "empty orchestra" accompaniment.
Prerecorded music fills the room,
and projection from a laser disc throws
a waterfall and red hibiscus onto the screen.
You are not interested in singing and
following the words as they change color
from yellow to purple across the cueing machine.
Instead, you walk out on blue-green glacier
ice and feel it thin to water in spring.
You notice two moose along the thawing shoreline
browsing for buds, and see the posted sign
"No shooting from here." But "here" is "there."

ICE FLOE

Nails dropped off a roof onto flagstone;
slow motion shatter of a windowpane;
the hushed sound when a circular saw cutting through plywood
stops, and splinters of wood are drifting in air;
lipstick graffiti on a living-room wall;
cold stinging your eardrums;
braking suddenly along a curve, and the car spinning,
holding your breath as the side-view mirror is snapped by a sign
  pole;
the snap as a purple chalk line marks an angular cut on black
  Cellutex;
dirt under your nails,
as you dig up green onions with your bare hands;
fiber plaster setting on a wall;
plugging in an iron and noticing the lights dim in the other room;
sound of a pencil drawn along the edge of a trisquare;
discovering your blurred vision is caused by having two contacts
  in each eye;
thud as the car slams into a snowbank and hits a fence;
smell of a burnt yam;
the bones of your wrist being crushed;
under a geranium leaf, a mass of spiders
moving slowly on tiny threads up and down and across to
  different stems.

THE LOS ALAMOS MUSEUM

In this museum is a replica of "Little Boy" and "Fat Man." In "Little Boy," a radar echo set off an explosive which drove a uranium-235 wedge into a larger uranium target, while in "Fat Man" the ordinary explosive crushed a hollow sphere of plutonium into a beryllium core. To the right of these replicas, a computer gives you the opportunity to design a reentry missile out of aluminum or steel. The reentry point of the aluminum missile needs to be thicker than the steel one, but, because it has a lighter atomic weight, when you push the button choosing the aluminum design, the computer rewards you with blinking lights and sounds. Further on in the main room, a model with lights shows the almost instantaneous release of neutrons and gamma rays from point zero. At point zero, radiant energy is released at the speed of light, but you can see it here in slow motion.

SPRING SNOW

A spring snow coincides with plum blossoms.
In a month, you will forget, then remember
when nine ravens perched in the elm sway in wind.

I will remember when I brake to a stop,
and a hubcap rolls through the intersection.
An angry man grinds pepper onto his salad;

it is how you nail a tin amulet ear
into the lintel. If, in deep emotion, we are
possessed by the idea of possession,

we can never lose to recover what is ours.
Sounds of an abacus are amplified and condensed
to resemble sounds of hail on a tin roof,

but mind opens to the smell of lightning.
Bodies were vaporized to shadows by intense heat;
in memory people outline bodies on walls.

O

THE REDSHIFTING WEB

1 The dragons on the back of a circular bronze mirror
swirl without end. I sit and am an absorbing form:
I absorb the outline of a snowy owl on a branch,
the rigor mortis in a hand. I absorb the crunching sounds
when you walk across a glacial lake with aquamarine
ice heaved up here and there twenty feet high.
I absorb the moment a jeweler pours molten gold
into a cuttlefish mold and it begins to smoke.
I absorb the weight of a pause when it tilts
the conversation in a room. I absorb the moments
he sleeps holding her right breast in his left hand
and know it resembles glassy waves in a harbor
in descending spring light. Is the mind a mirror?
I see pig carcasses piled up from the floor
on a boat docked at Wanxian and the cook
who smokes inadvertently drops ashes into soup.
I absorb the stench of burning cuttlefish bone,
and as moments coalesce see to travel far is to return.

2 A cochineal picker goes blind;

Mao, swimming across the Yangtze River,
was buoyed by underwater frogmen;

in the nursing home,
she yelled, "Everyone here has Alzheimer's!"

it blistered his mouth;

they thought the tape of *erhu* solos was a series of spy messages;

finding a bag of piki pushpinned to the door;

shapes of saguaros by starlight;

a yogi tries on cowboy boots at a flea market;

a peregrine falcon
shears off a wing;

her niece went through the house and took what she wanted;

"The sooner the better";

like a blindman grinding the bones of a snow leopard;

she knew you had come to cut her hair;

suffering: this and that:
iron 26, gold 79;

they dared him to stare at the annular eclipse;

the yellow pupils of a saw-whet owl.

3 The gold shimmer at the beginning of summer
dissolves in a day. A fly mistakes a
gold spider, the size of a pinhead, at the center
of a glistening web. A morning mushroom
knows nothing of twilight and dawn?
Instead of developing a navy, Ci Xi
ordered architects to construct a two-story
marble boat that floats on a lotus-covered lake.
Mistake a death cap for Caesar's amanita
and in hours a hepatic hole opens into the sky.
To avoid yelling at his pregnant wife,
a neighbor installs a boxing bag in a storeroom;
he periodically goes in, punches, punches,
reappears and smiles. A hummingbird moth
hovers and hovers at a woman wearing a
cochineal-dyed flowery dress. Liu Hansheng
collects hypodermic needles, washes them
under a hand pump, dries them in sunlight,
seals them in Red Cross plastic bags,
resells them as sterilized new ones to hospitals.

4 Absorb a corpse-like silence and be a brass
cone at the end of a string beginning
to mark the x of stillness. You may puzzle
as to why a meson beam oscillates, or why
galaxies appear to be simultaneously redshifting
in all directions, but do you stop to sense
death pulling and pulling from the center
of the earth to the end of the string?
A mother screams at her son, "You're so stupid,"
but the motion of this anger is a circle.
A teen was going to attend a demonstration,
but his parents, worried about tear gas,
persuaded him to stay home: he was bludgeoned
to death that afternoon by a burglar.
I awake dizzy with a searing headache
thinking what nightmare did I have
that I cannot remember only to discover
the slumlord dusted the floor with roach powder.

5 Moored off Qingdao, before sunrise,
the pilot of a tanker is selling dismantled bicycles.
Once, a watchmaker coated numbers on the dial

with radioactive paint and periodically
straightened the tip of the brush in his mouth.
Our son sights the North Star through a straw

taped to a protractor so that a bolt
dangling from a string marks the latitude.
I remember when he said his first word, "Clock";

his 6:02 is not mine, nor is your 7:03 his.
We visit Aurelia in the nursing home and find
she is sleeping curled in a fetal position.

A chain-smoking acupuncturist burps, curses;
a teen dips his head in paint thinner.
We think, had I *this* then that would,

but subjunctive form is surge and ache.
Yellow tips of chamisa are flaring open.
I drop a jar of mustard, and it shatters in a wave.

6 The smell of roasted chili;

descending into the epilimnion;

the shape of a datura leaf;

a bank robber superglued his fingertips;

in the lake,
ocean-seal absorption;

a moray snaps up a scorpion fish;

he had to mistake and mistake;

burned popcorn;

he lifted the fly agaric off of blue paper
and saw a white galaxy;

sitting in a cold sweat;

a child drinking Coke out of a formula bottle
has all her teeth capped in gold;

chrysanthemum-shaped fireworks exploding over the water;

red piki passed down a ladder;

laughter;

as a lobster mold transforms a russula into a delicacy;

replicating an Anasazi
yucca fiber and turkey-feather blanket.

7 He looks at a series of mirrors: Warring States,
Western Han, Eastern Han, Tang, Song,
and notices bits of irregular red corrosion

on the Warring States mirror. On the back,
three dragons swirl in mist and April air.
After sixteen years that first kiss

still has a flaring tail. He looks at the TLV
pattern on the back of the Han mirror:
the mind has diamond points east, south, west, north.

He grimaces and pulls up a pile of potatoes,
notices snow clouds coming in from the west.
She places a sunflower head on the northwest

corner of the fence. He looks at the back
of the Tang mirror: the lion and grape
pattern is so wrought he turns, watches her

pick eggplant, senses the underlying
twist of pleasure and surprise that
in mind they flow and respond endlessly.

8 I find a rufous hummingbird on the floor
of a greenhouse, sense a redshifting
along the radial string of a web.
You may draw a cloud pattern in cement
setting in a patio, or wake to
sparkling ferns melting on a windowpane.
The struck, plucked, bowed, blown
sounds of the world come and go.
As first light enters a telescope
and one sees light of a star when the star
has vanished, I see a finch at a feeder,
beans germinating in darkness;
a man with a pole pulls yarn out
of an indigo vat, twists and untwists it;
I hear a shout as a child finds *Boletus*
barrowsii under ponderosa pine;
I see you wearing an onyx-and-gold pin.
In curved space, is a line a circle?

9 Pausing in the motion of a stroke,
two right hands
grasping a brush;

staring through a skylight
at a lunar eclipse;

a great blue heron,
wings flapping,
landing on the rail of a float house;

near and far:
a continuous warp;

a neighbor wants to tear down this fence;
a workman covets it
for a *trastero*;

raccoons on the rooftop
eating apricots;

the character *xuan* –
dark, dyed –
pinned to a wall above a computer;

lovers making
a room glow;

weaving on a vertical loom:
sound of a comb,
baleen;

hiding a world in a world:
1054, a supernova.

X RAY

In my mind a lilac begins to leaf

before it begins to leaf.
A new leaf

is a new moon.
As the skin of a chameleon

reflects temperature, light, emotion,
an X ray of my hands

reflects chance, intention, hunger?
You can, in X ray
diffraction,
study the symmetry of crystals,

but here, now,
the caesura marks a shift in the mind,

the vicissitudes
of starlight,

a luna moth opening its wings.

RATTLESNAKE GLYPH

Curve of the earth in emerald water
deepening into blue where water breaks along

the outer edge of a reef. A snake of equinoctial
light is beginning to descend the nine tiers

of a pyramid. You hear a shout reverberate
down the walls of a ball court, find blood

snakes spurting out of the neck of a decapitated man,
the carved stone ring through which a human head

used as a ball must pass. Here is a wall of
a thousand white sculptured-stone skulls

and row after row of heads mounted on spikes.
The darkness drops a mosquito net over a bed:

in blood scroll skull light, I taste the salt
on your skin and in your hair. We are

a rattlesnake glyph aligning memory, dream, desire.
At dawn the slashing sounds of rain turn out

to be wind in the palms. Waves are breaking white
on the reef. Soon turtles will arrive and lay

eggs in the sand. A line of leaf-cutting ants
are passing bits of shiny green leaves across a trail.

A GREAT SQUARE HAS NO CORNERS

"Cut."
An actress feigning death for one hundred seconds gasps.
A man revs
and races a red Mustang up and down the street.
"Cut."

A potter opens a hillside kiln;
he removes a molten bowl,
and, dipping it
in cold water,
it hisses, turns black, cracks.

In despair, a pearl is a sphere.
"Cut."
In Bombay, a line of ear cleaners are standing in a street.
On a mesa top,
the south windows of a house shatter;

underground uranium miners
are releasing explosives.
"Cut."
A rope beginning to unravel in the mind
is, like red antlers,

the axis of a dream.
"Cut."
What is the secret to stopping time?
A one-eyed calligrapher
writes with a mop, "A great square has no corners."

AXOLOTL

I may practice divination with the bones
of an eel, but the world would be
just as cruel were it within my will.

The yellowing leaves of the honey locust
would still be yellowing, and a woman
riding in a hearse would still grieve and grieve.

We don't live in a hypothetical world,
and yet the world would be nothing
without hypothetical dreaming. I hope no

ultimate set of laws to nature exists;
maybe, instead, there's only layering.
Maybe you look in a store window and see

twenty-four televisions with twenty-four images:
now the explosion of a napalm bomb,
now the face of an axolotl.

MUSHROOM HUNTING IN THE JEMEZ MOUNTAINS

Walking in a mountain meadow toward the north slope,
I see redcap amanitas with white warts and know
they signal cèpes. I see a few colonies of puffballs,
red russulas with chalk-white stipes, brown-gilled
Poison Pie. In the shade under spruce are two
red-pored boletes: slice them in half and the flesh
turns blue in seconds. Under fir is a single amanita
with basal cup, flaring annulus, white cap: is it
the Rocky Mountain form of *Amanita pantherina*?
I am aware of danger in naming, in misidentification,
in imposing the distinctions of a taxonomic language
onto the things themselves. I know I have only
a few hours to hunt mushrooms before early afternoon rain.
I know it is a mistake to think I am moving and
that agarics are still: they are more transient
than we acknowledge, more susceptible to full moon,
to a single rain, to night air, to a moment of sunshine.
I know in this meadow my passions are mycorrhizal
with nature. I may shout out ecstasies, aches, griefs,
and hear them vanish in the white-pored silence.

FROM THE ROOFTOP

He wakes up to the noise of ravens in the spruce trees.
For a second, in the mind, the parsley is already
bolting in the heat, but then he realizes
the mind focusing rays into a burning point of light
can also relax its intensity, and then
he feels the slow wave of the day.
Mullein growing by the gas meter
is as significant as the portulaca blooming in pots.
Ants are marching up the vine onto the stucco wall
and into the roof. From the rooftop,
he contemplates the pattern of lightning to the west,
feels a nine-pointed buck edge closer to the road at dusk,
weighs a leaf and wonders what is significant,
maybe the neighbor who plays the saxophone
at odd hours, loudly and badly, but with such expanse.

THE SHAPES OF LEAVES

Ginkgo, cottonwood, pin oak, sweet gum, tulip tree:
our emotions resemble leaves and alive
to their shapes we are nourished.

Have you felt the expanse and contours of grief
along the edges of a big Norway maple?
Have you winced at the orange flare

searing the curves of a curling dogwood?
I have seen from the air logged islands,
each with a network of branching gravel roads,

and felt a moment of pure anger, aspen gold.
I have seen sandhill cranes moving in an open field,
a single white whooping crane in the flock.

And I have traveled along the contours
of leaves that have no name. Here
where the air is wet and the light is cool,

I feel what others are thinking and do not speak,
I know pleasure in the veins of a sugar maple,
I am living at the edge of a new leaf.

O

ORIGINAL MEMORY

1 White orchids along the window –
she notices something has nibbled the eggplant leaves,

mantises have not yet hatched from the egg.
"*Traduttori, traditori,*" said a multilinguist

discussing the intricacies of Hopi time and space,
but the inadvertent resonance in the mind

is that passion is original memory:
she is at the window pointing to Sagittarius,

she is slicing *porcini* and laying them in a pan,
she is repotting a cereus wearing chalcedony-and-gold earrings,

she is judging kachinas and selecting the simplest
to the consternation of museum employees.

Grilled shrimp in olive oil –
a red sensation pours into his thought and touch:

the sfumato of her face,
shining black hair reaching down to her waist,

he knows without looking the plum
bruises on her thigh from the spikes of a sectional warp.

2 The multilinguist wants to reveal the locations
of shrines on the salt trail in the Grand Canyon

but has been declared persona non grata by the tribe.
He may have disproved the thesis that the Hopi language

has no referents to time, but his obsession led
to angers and accusations, betrayals and pentimenti:

a cry of a nuthatch vanishes into aquamarine air.
Some things you have to see by making a pinhole,

holding a white sheet of paper at the proper focal length?
To try to retrace the arc of a passion is to

try to dream in slow motion a bursting into flame?
You are collecting budding yellow tea plants;

I am feeling a sexual splendor in a new orchid leaf.
What is the skin of the mind?

How do you distinguish "truth" from "true perception"?
When is an apex a nadir and a nadir an opening into a first world?

Italians slice *porcini*, lay them on screens in the sun,
let the maggots wriggle out and drop to the ground.

3 She is tipping water out of a cloud.
By candlelight, face to face,

the pleasures of existence are caught in a string of pearls.
He remembers her rhythm in a corn dance,

notices the swelling of her left ear from a new earring.
He does not want any distortion –

red leaves falling or beginning to fall,
bright yellow chamisa budding along a dirt road,

snow accumulating on black branches –
to this moment of chiaroscuro in which their lives are a sphere.

Face to face, by candlelight,
the rock work and doorways form a series of triptychs.

She remembers hiking the trail up to Peñasco Blanco,
sees the Chuska Mountains violet in the west,

and, below, the swerve of Chaco Wash,
the canyon opening up: ruins of rock walls

calcined in the heat, and, in red light,
swallows gathering and daubing mud along the cliff face.

O

ARCHIPELAGO

1 I walk along the length of a stone-and-gravel garden
and feel without looking how the fifteen stones
appear and disappear. I had not expected the space
to be defined by a wall made of clay boiled in oil
nor to see above a series of green cryptomeria
pungent in spring. I stop and feel an April snow
begin to fall on the stones and raked gravel and see
how distance turns into abstraction desire and ordinary
things: from the air, corn and soybean fields are
a series of horizontal and vertical stripes of pure color:
viridian, yellow ocher, raw sienna, sap green. I
remember in Istanbul at the entrance to the Blue Mosque
two parallel, extended lines of shoes humming at
the threshold of paradise. Up close, it's hard to know
if the rattle of milk bottles will become a topaz,
or a moment of throttled anger tripe that is
chewed and chewed. In the distance, I feel drumming
and chanting and see a line of Pueblo women dancing
with black-on-black jars on their heads; they lift
the jars high then start to throw them to the ground.

2 Rope at ankle level,
a walkway sprinkled with water
under red and orange maples along a white-plastered wall;

moss covering the irregular ground
under propped-up weeping cherry trees;

in a corral
a woman is about to whisper and pat the roan's neck;

an amber chasm inside a cello;

in a business conversation,
the silences are eel farms passed on a bullet train;

a silence in the shape of a rake;

a sheet of ice floating along a dock;
the texture of icy-black basil leaves at sunrise;

a shaggymane pushing up through asphalt;

a woman wearing a multicolored dress of silk-screened naked women
about to peel an egg;

three stones leading into a pond.

3 Desire is to memory as an azalea is to a stone?
During the Cultural Revolution, the youngest brother
of the Peng family was executed against a wall
in Chengdu for being a suspected Guomindang agent.
Years earlier, the eldest brother was executed
at that wall for being a suspected communist.
This Chengdu effect has no end, but if you interiorize,
a series of psychological tragedies
has the resonance of stone-and-gravel waterfalls.
A first frost sweetens the apples; I want them sweeter
but discover a second frost makes the cores mush;
so essential shapes are destroyed starting at the center.
A woman and man must ache from a series of betrayals
before they can begin to bicker at the dinner table.
I water hyacinth bulbs planted in shallow pots
in the cool, dark bathroom, and, though it feels
odd to do so when walnuts are rotting on the ground,
a thought of spring is inadvertent pleasure:
a policeman pushed a dancer against a car, said, "Sure,"
when he insisted he had marigolds, not marijuana.

4 She puts jars in a pit, covers them with sawdust,
adds a layer of shards and covers them,
builds a fire, and, when the burn is intense,
smothers it with sheep dung. She will not know
for a few hours if the jars have turned completely
black and did not break cooling. For now,
no one sees or knows; I inhale smoke, see
vendors along the docks selling grilled
corn smelling of charcoal, the air at dusk
plangent with cries from minarets up on the hill –
the cries resembling the waves of starlings
that always precede the pulsing wing-beat Vs
of sandhill cranes. Oh, you can glow with anger,
but it leaves the soot of an oil burner
on the windows and walls. If anguish is an end
in itself, you walk into a landscape of
burned salt cedar along a river. I remember
seeing hungry passengers disembark at the docks.

5 Men dressed in cottonwood leaves dance
in the curving motion of a green rattlesnake.
I am walking along a sandstone trail
and stop in a field of shards: here is a teal zigzag
and there is a blood-red deer's breath-arrow.
Women dancers offer melons to the six directions
then throw them to the ground. A wave
rocks through the crowd as the melons are smashed open.
I know I have walked along a path lit
by candles inside open-mesh cast-iron carp.
I stop at a water basin, and as I bend to
ladle water, see reflected, a sweet gum leaf.
As a cornmeal path becomes a path to the gods
then a cornmeal path again, I see the line
of women dancing with black-on-black jars on their heads.
They raise the jars with macaw and lightning patterns
to the six directions then form a circle
and throw them down on the center-marking stones.

6 "Go kiss a horse's ass."

"He hanged himself from the flagpole."

"I just do what I'm told."

She wanted him to hold her and say nothing.

"Depression is due to loss or guilt."

Who heard shrieks?
In the morning,
a mutilated body was found behind the adobe church.

He saw that "A or B" was not a choice since A and B had predetermined.

"I hated that painting painting so I burned it."

Hair on the woodstove.

"I'm so glad."

After fallopian surgery, she touches her scar, combs her hair, puts on makeup.

The red phoenix tattoos on the arms of a locksmith.

"A man's character is his fate."

He had two cameras but was always pawning one to release the
other.

They slept a Mediterranean sleep: sun, sand, water;
the bed had the soft motion of waves.

"No, no, no, no, no, no, no!"

"Water is the koan of water."

7 I look at fourteen stones submerged at varying depths
in a sea of gravel. I do not know under which stone
is a signature but guess that a pin-sized hourglass space,
separating intention and effect, is a blind point
where anger may coalesce into a pearl. I may sit here
until the stones have a riparian shine and are buoyant
in September starlight, yet never live to see
how grief turns into the effortless stretch of a fisherman
casting a fly onto a stream. When I slept on the float house
I became accustomed to the rise and fall of the tide,
so that when I walked on the rain forest island
I was queasy. I wanted a still pellucid point
but realize the necessary and sufficient condition
is to feel the pin-sized space as a point of resistance,
as a smash that is a beginning wave of light.
The dancers reappear and enter the plaza in two lines.
Shifting feet in rhythm to the shifting drumming,
they approach the crowd under the yellow cottonwood.

8 Mating above the cattails, red dragonflies –

sipping litchi tea, eating fried scallion pancakes –

bamboo slivers under the fingernails –

playing Ping-Pong by candlelight in a greenhouse –

digging up and rotating soil in the flower beds –

pulling and pulling at her throat until it bleeds –

scraping the skin of the earth –

finding shaggymanes have deliquesced into black ink –

releasing endorphins in the brain –

archipelago:
an expanse of water with many scattered islands –

a python coiling around sixteen white oblong eggs –

waking in the dark to pungent hyacinths –

blooming the pure white curve of blooming –

dancers are throwing
licorice, sunflower seeds, pot scrubbers, aprons, plastic bowls.

9 Plastic bowls, aprons, pot scrubbers, sunflower seeds, licorice –

the shadow of a hummingbird –

crab apple blossoms scattering in the street –

a silence in the shape of a chanterelle –

a turkey feather hanging from a branch of mountain ash –

the forms of lightning –

a yellow iris blooming near the house marker, 1932 –

river stones marking the noon solstice –

black, *blak*, *blaec* –

following the thread
of recollection through a lifetime –

the passions becoming the chiming sounds of jade –

blue corn growing in a field of sand –

the *chug chug*, *ka ka* of a cactus wren –

a black-and-yellow butterfly closing then opening its wings –

egrets wading in shallow water at low tide.

NOTES

page 10 Man On Horseback: the *Tricholoma flavovirens* mushroom

10 s twist, z twist: threads of fiber may be spun in either an s-spin (counterclockwise) or z-spin (clockwise) direction

13 chamisa: in the Southwest, another name for rabbitbrush

15 catalog of endangered species

23 *kaiseki*: (Japanese) breast stones; a Zen meal that accompanies tea ceremony

23 Qianlong: Chinese emperor 1736–1799

24 Daruma: the founder of Zen

26 *Tokpela*: (Hopi) sky, the name of the first world

26 *trastero*: in the Southwest, a cupboard

28 *feng shui*: (Chinese) wind and water; the art of balancing and enhancing the environment

28 Two Grey Hills: a style of Navajo weaving

31 *matcha*: (Japanese) a powdered green tea

38 *kukui*: Hawaiian name for the candlenut tree

43 *huan wo he shan*: (Chinese) return my rivers and mountains

46 *'apapane, 'i'iwi*: names of Hawaiian birds

49 *o'o a'a*: Hawaiian bird

83 *ristras*: in the Southwest, strings, e.g., of chili

97 *canal*: a waterspout off a roof

97 *vigas*: ceiling beams

97 *latillas*: stripped aspen poles laid across ceiling beams

106 questa: a small town in northern New Mexico

165 *Kooyemsi*: (Hopi) mudhead kachinas

175 *kwakwha*: (Hopi) thank you (*masc*)

175 *askwali*: (Hopi) thank you (*fem*)

186 *enso*: in Zen calligraphy, the circle

193 *shibui*: (Japanese) astringent, refined

194 *karez*: irrigation tunnels

213 *chacmool*: (Mayan) a reclining human figure with flexed knees, head turned to the side, hands holding a basin at the navel

224 *erhu*: a Chinese two-stringed fiddle

224 piki: (Hopi) bread made especially from blue cornmeal and baked in thin sheets

231 TLV: in the Han dynasty, a series of so-called TLV mirrors appeared; the backs of these mirrors have geomantic forms resembling the letters T, L, V

233 *xuan*: the Chinese character means dark, deep, profound, subtle, and is etymologically derived from dyeing

247 *traduttori, traditori*: (Italian) translators, traitors

262 *blak, blaec*: the Middle English and Old English spellings of *black*

ABOUT THE AUTHOR

ARTHUR SZE is a second-generation Chinese American who was born in New York City in 1950. He graduated Phi Beta Kappa from the University of California at Berkeley and is the author of six books of poetry. His poems have appeared in numerous magazines and anthologies, and have been translated into Chinese and Italian. He has taught at Brown University, Bard College, and the Naropa Institute, and is the recipient of numerous awards, including a John Simon Guggenheim Memorial Foundation Fellowship, a Lila Wallace–*Reader's Digest* Writer's Award, a Lannan Literary Award for Poetry, and fellowships from the Witter Bynner Foundation for Poetry and the National Endowment for the Arts, among many others. He currently lives in Pojoaque, New Mexico, with his wife, Carol Moldaw, and is a Professor of Creative Writing at the Institute of American Indian Arts.

Book design & composition by John D. Berry, using PageMaker 6.5 on a Power 120 and a Power Macintosh G3. The type is Minion multiple master, designed by Robert Slimbach as part of the Adobe Originals type library. Minion is derived from no single source, but is based on typefaces of the late Renaissance. Slimbach designed Minion in 1990, then expanded it in 1992 to become a multiple master font – the first to include a size axis for optical scaling. *Printed by Bang Printing.*